Shurik

Shurik

A WWII SAGA OF THE SIEGE OF LENINGRAD

Kyra Petrovskaya Wayne

With an Introduction by
Harrison E. Salisbury

THE LYONS PRESS

For my grandchildren Nicholas, Christopher, Emily
and Natalie Wayne, with all my love, hoping that they
would be spared the horrors of wars, starvation and despair.

Printed in Canada

Originally published by Grosset & Dunlap, 1970

10 9 8 7 6 5 4 3 2

Library of Congress Cataloging-in-Publication Data

Wayne, Kyra Petrovskaya.
    Shurik : a WWII saga of the siege of Leningrad / by Kyra Petrovskaya
Wayne ; with an introduction by Harrison E. Salisbury.
        p.   cm.
    Summary: A Russian actress and nurse tells of her experience
caring for an orphan boy during part of the three-year siege of
Leningrad.
    ISBN 1-58574-176-0 : $14.95
    [1. Leningrad (R.S.F.S.R)—History—Siege, 1941–1944
2. Nikanorov, Shurik. 3. Wayne, Kyra Petrovskaya.] I. Title.
D764.3.L4W38 1992
940.53'47453'092—dc20   91-44325
                                                             CIP
                                                             AC

AUTHOR'S NOTE

Fifty years have passed since the events described in this book took place. I am a grandmother now and my eldest grandson, Nicky, is of exactly the same age as was Shurik when I first found him.

Monumental changes have taken place during this half century. My beloved city, Leningrad, is once again St. Petersburg, the city of Peter the Great, whose statue still rises on the granite banks of the Neva river. But the name—Leningrad—will forever be engraved in history for the heroic struggle of its people against aggression during the nine-hundred-day siege.

I am one of the survivors of that siege. I sift through my memories with sadness and pride. I think of my beautiful, gentle mother, who had died a brutal death during the siege. I think of my many friends, all fallen either on a battlefield or killed by starvation in the blockaded city. And, as I look at my medal *For the Defense of Leningrad*, I think of those who survived, those lucky ones like Shurik and myself. And, of course, I think of Shurik. What has become of him? Does he ever think of me?

I live in the United States now, having married an American who took me out of Russia so many years ago. As I watch on television or read about the fast changes taking place in the Soviet Union, I rejoice that the country of my birth is once again a friend of the country of my choice.

I am content now, writing books, surrounded by a loving family, my dogs and cats and flowers in my garden. The past, the days of the siege, now seem almost unreal in the midst of my American life. But I don't want to forget those days. I want my grandchildren to know about them, to live them through this book and to appreciate their own lives in a peaceful country.

Let's hope that *they* will never have to experience the kind of life Shurik led during those tragic and heroic days. As a Leningrad poet said in those times, "let no one forget, let nothing be forgotten."

INTRODUCTION

On June 3, 1943, the poetess Vera Inber, a Moscow woman who had of her own free choice gone to Leningrad and there endured the great siege, was presented with the medal "For the Defense of Leningrad." She noted in her diary that "this little metal disc joins to itself all of Leningrad."

The Soviet government presented the medal to every resident of Leningrad who survived the 900-day siege. Exactly how many were passed out has never been revealed. But the number should have been in the range of 1,500,000 or a bit more, depending on the criteria employed. There were about 2,500,000 persons in Leningrad when the siege began in September.

There is no reason to believe that the Soviet government did not act with sincerity in distributing the awards with their green-and-red ribbon and their German-silver medallion. So far as I know no effort was made to give the medal to another 1,000,000 or possibly 1,300,000 Leningraders who remained in the great northern city. These were the dead; the dead whose number in all conscience is beyond counting; a total which never will be known with exactitude and which, it might be noted, has become the subject of new and painful argument among Soviet writers, historians and propagandists, as a result of the publication of my own work on the siege, *The 900 Days*. The details of the argument are not important but the essence of the matter is that the Government even after 25 years simply cannot bring itself to admit the magnitude of the catastrophe.

Of course, the question of exactly how many died in Leningrad has long since been moot from the standpoint of principle. One-third of a great city? Half of a great city? When the numbers run so large they become meaningless. What is important is not whether the number is, as the Soviet government originally estimated it for purposes of the Nuremberg war crimes trial, 632,253, or something like twice that. What is important is that no city in modern times, no group of civilians anywhere in the world under any circumstances, has been subjected to an ordeal like that of Leningrad—nearly 900 days under Nazi siege, much of the time cut off from all but the most marginal connection with the rest of Russia. And during that time Leningrad endured winter cold that dropped to 40 below zero in buildings that were without heat or light; drew water from the frozen Neva river (for all the pipes and plumbing and sewers in the city were frozen); had no transportation, neither street cars, busses nor cars; lay buried in snow that sometimes reached to second story windows; starved on rations that dwindled to two slices of bread a day— made from flour which was often a mixture of sawdust, flour dust sweepings from old millfloors, rotten barley, cellulose and bark. Leningrad was a city where corpses lay so thick in some streets that pedestrians had to detour around them; a city where the dead lay unattended in almost every frozen apartment; a city where the loudest noise was the squeak of runners of children's sleds, bearing the dead to morgues and cemeteries.

It was a city of dread where gunmen preyed on weakened citizens and cannibals were said to lurk in alleys near the black markets, lying in wait for victims.

It was a city of fear. But it was also a city of heroes. Never in human history did men and women and children give so freely of their courage, their spirit and their love. Horror and heroism— these are the qualities of the Leningrad epic and the heroism will inspire the world as long as the story is told of the brave men and women of Leningrad.

Kyra Petrovskaya was of that golden band of heroes, one of the company of the brave who endured Leningrad, who went through its hell and emerged, like so many others, to live her life in circumstances which we can describe as normal and even ordinary. But she has forgotten nothing of the days in Leningrad. With Olga Berggoltz she can say: "Let no one forget; let nothing be forgotten."

She has written the tale of a Leningrad youngster whom she befriended when she was a nurse during the Leningrad siege in one of the great Leningrad hospitals. I suppose one might say, as well, that Shurik befriended her and Dr. Stern, the outwardly gruff, inwardly tender chief of Military Hospital No. 902 where Kyra Petrovskaya worked.

Shurik was a youngster who had lost his father at the front and his mother under the bombed rubble of an apartment house where Kyra Petrovskaya found him digging stubbornly in the ruins. She took him in. Shurik's life was saved and in the saving he helped to save other lives and give others spirit to withstand the terrors of the ordeal.

In the annals of Leningrad the story of Shurik and Kyra Petrovskaya has a familiar ring. It is not too different from a hundred stories of youngsters and adults who helped each other to survive. But that is what makes the story so warm and so touching. It is drawn from the commonbook of Leningrad. I think it will bring to the American reader something of the warmth, the tenderness, the nearness, the intimacy which only those who lived so close to death could share.

In small scale the story of Shurik and Kyra Petrovskaya *is* the story of Leningrad. I do not know whether Kyra Petrovskaya was awarded the medal for the defense of Leningrad. I do not know whether Shurik was so honored. No matter. To have lived in Leningrad during those days; to have endured; to have survived; to have emerged—this is honor enough. No medal made of metal, no matter how precious, can serve to pay humanity's tribute to the people of Leningrad. One can only echo with that magnificent Leningrad poet, Yuri Voronov:

> Let this tale live forever
> In our hearts, forever heard!
> Let its memory be our conscience.

—Harrison E. Salisbury

The author's first year as a lieutenant on the Leningrad front. *Author's photo*

1

There has never been such a cold winter before, I thought as I trotted down the middle of the icy street. The soles of my military boots thumped against snow packed hard as stone, creating a feeling of "pins and needles" in my frozen toes. The sensation was almost pleasant, for it made me feel warmer.

I thought with longing of my cozy room a short distance away. In a few minutes I would start a fire in my ceramic stove with the shelves from my bookcase. The shelves were made of stained mahogany, dry and heavy. They would keep me warm for a while.

In the distance I heard the explosion of an artillery shell. It was another of the shells that had fallen upon Leningrad at random, for more than three months. Day and night one heard the deep, booming explosions, which spared no part of the city.

One more turn and I'll be home, I thought. I was ravenously hungry. I had been on duty for twelve hours and had eaten my daily bowl of soup standing up, at the nurses' station. I was tired, too. The Military Hospital No. 902—housed in a modern school building where I worked as a nurse—overflowed with wounded soldiers who kept arriving daily in great convoys of camouflaged trucks. At times we had to leave the soldiers in the trucks for a full day before beds became available in the hospital. We would give the men first aid and cover them with all the blankets we could spare, hoping that none would freeze to death before we could bring them inside. Some did freeze. I'll always remember the first time I found a soldier frozen to death. The man might have died from the loss of blood anyway, but there was something especially horrible about his dying when he was so close to being saved.

A few more buildings to pass and I would be home. Home, until tomorrow, in the warmth of my own little room, baking potatoes in the hot coals of my stove, reading Hemingway in the flickering light of a candle. If I were lucky, there might be an hour or two of electric light. One never knew.

One more apartment house to pass or, rather, the ruins of a house. It had been hit by a shell only two days before. It must have been a huge shell, for the whole building had been destroyed. The explosion had shaken the entire neighborhood, shattering some windows in my apartment house and breaking my set of crystal glasses. Fortunately the windows in my room remained intact. Once broken, they could not be replaced.

As I passed the house, I looked at it again. My school friend, Nadya, used to live there. I wondered where she was now. Probably somewhere at the front. The last time I had seen her was during the summer, when we both were graduating from a *druzhinniza* class. She looked smart in her uniform with the field-nurse arm band and medical corps emblem on her military cap.

Once I was envious of her. She had been assigned to front-line duty immediately, while I had been detained to take an additional course to become a hospital nurse. I wanted to go to the front. All my friends were there, fighting. And I felt that by staying behind and studying at the school of nursing, I was betraying my country. While my friends were constantly risking their lives, I learned to take the pulse and give an enema! But that was during the first months of the war, before Leningrad came under siege. Now, in November, the very streets of the city became the front lines. The bombardment of the city never stopped. Our patients at the hospital were only half joking when they complained that they felt safer at the front-line positions. There, at least, they could hide in their foxholes and wait until the worst was over. In the city they felt trapped behind the thin walls of the hospital. The shriek of bombs and the sound of long-range guns deprived our patients of sleep and made them nervous and restless.

I glanced at the demolished house again. There were four stories of apartments, neatly sliced in half like a dollhouse. I could see the remaining half of the rooms, as if they were part of a stage set. There were curtains on one window, and someone's coat on a nail gently swayed in the wind. In another room a baby grand piano stood precariously in a corner.

Something attracted my attention to a pile of brick rubble at the foot of the bombed house. I thought I saw some movement. It was always possible that the Civil Defense Corps, which searched in the tumbled ruins for survivors, had overlooked someone. There were so many ruins, so many victims. I climbed over the pile of bricks, slippery under the freshly fallen snow.

"Anybody there?" I called.

"Yes. It's me, Shurik." A child's voice came faintly from the rubble in the depths of the shell crater.

"Are you hurt?" I cried.

"I'm so cold" was the reply. There was scratching and puffing, and in a few moments a small, dirty figure covered with powdery red-brick dust stood in front of me.

"Who are you? What's your name?" I asked.

"Shurik Nikanorov," replied the boy. He couldn't have been more than ten.

"What were you doing there?"

"I used to live there."

"But what were you doing there just now?" I insisted.

"I was looking for my mother. She must be there—somewhere. She was home when the house was hit. She must be there. Maybe she was in the shelter. I must find her," the boy babbled, as if in delirium.

I took his thin wrist in my hand and felt his pulse. It raced wildly. The child was feverish.

"Come with me," I said. "It's getting too dark to see anything now. We'll look for your mother in the morning." Obediently Shurik put his cold, clawlike hand into mine.

"Here, put these on." I took my mittens off and handed them to Shurik. He tried to put them on, but his frozen fingers didn't obey him. He dropped the mittens.

"Let me help you," I said. One glance at the ruined building was enough to tell me that his mother must have been killed or wounded during the bombing. The civil defense workers had probably removed her body, either to a hospital or to a morgue.

"Where is your father?"

"At the front. He is a sergeant. A gunner in a tank battalion," Shurik answered, his teeth chattering.

"Do you have any other family? Grandparents, perhaps, or brothers or sisters?"

"No. My mother told me that I would have a little brother or sister in February."

Poor woman, I thought. My hands felt cold without mittens, but I couldn't release Shurik. Half supporting him with one hand, I stuck the other inside my military overcoat in Napoleonlike fashion, opening and closing my fingers to keep the circulation going.

"Just a few more steps," I said, mostly for my own benefit. Shurik was silent. He followed me trustingly, as if he had known me all his life.

"Here we are. Now, I must light a match so we won't stumble in the dark." The matches were damp and refused to burn. I broke several before I was able to light one, which sputtered and crackled and promptly went out. But these scant seconds of light were enough to see a corpse, lying at the foot of the steps. *Another one,* I thought, as Shurik and I stepped over it and began our ascent to my flat on the fourth floor. This was the third body I had seen at the foot of the stairs within the week. In the morning—hopefully—it would be gone. The civil defense workers would remove it for burial.

I fumbled for my key and opened the door of my apartment. It was almost as cold as outdoors. We staggered in the dark through a communal kitchen, once filled with the laughter of the housewives who shared it. Now it was deserted. Most of the tenants had been mobilized into defense units, and those who remained huddled in their own rooms, preferring to cook their scanty meals on their own stoves like I did, guarding their precious food supplies from one another.

We stopped in front of my door. With another key, I opened a heavy padlock. At one time I left my room unlocked. Now it was impossible. My food, my wood, my water supply—everything would surely be stolen by my desperate neighbors.

It was warmer in my room. The embers in my ceramic stove still glowed a bit.

"Don't take your coat off until I start the fire," I said to Shurik. "Sit down." Passively he sank to the floor from exactly where he was standing. I stumbled in the dark until I found a candle and a box of good, pre-war matches. The flickering candlelight made the room seem more cheerful.

"Sit on the sofa," I said to Shurik. "It's less cold there." Like a little robot he changed his place. I used pages from the *Great Soviet Atlas* to kindle the fire. This volume had seen me through many years at school, and now it helped me to survive my nineteenth year of life. On top of the paper went my bookshelves. The shelves caught at once. Next, the case itself would have to be burned, board by board, molding by molding.

I turned to Shurik. He was covered with brick dust from head to foot. I couldn't see his face, only two bright, feverish eyes.

"While our potatoes roast, I'll clean you up. You look like a red Indian." I tried to make him smile, but he merely stared.

I turned back to the stove and made a hollow in the coals under the grate and buried four potatoes there. "All right," I said, "soon our supper will be ready." I took my overcoat off and rolled up the sleeves of my military tunic.

"Now, Shurik, let me see your face. Take your hat off." He took his warm, fur-flapped hat off. His hair—pale-blond, matted and in need of combing—looked like a wig stuck on a red-faced mannequin.

"I don't have much water. We must save it for drinking. But, fortunately, I have a whole jar of vaseline. We'll remove all this dirt just like actors do when they remove their make-up," I said, reaching into my dressing table for vaseline and cotton. Shurik waited, listlessly. I took his dirty clothes off and wrapped him in my old terry-cloth bathrobe. He shivered.

"Sit here, by the fire." I moved a chair in front of the open door of the stove. The heat came out in waves, and the room began to feel warm.

"Close your eyes and don't open them until I say so. We don't want vaseline in your eyes," I said, beginning the painstaking job of cleaning him up. Oh, to have a bathtub, full of hot, soapy water!

"Where were you when the house was bombed?" I asked casually. "Keep your eyes shut!"

"I was at the river, with my sled. Mother had sent me for water."

How well I knew the task! All the pipes in the city were solidly frozen. Everyone had to get their water from the river. There were always crowds of women and children with their sleds and containers, waiting beside holes in the ice to take turns dipping the muddy water. It was a slippery, dangerous job.

"So?" I prompted Shurik to continue.

"So, I came home—and the house was gone. There were people and firemen yelling and running around. I got scared. I ran away. Later, when the firemen were gone, I returned and started searching for my mother."

"But the house was bombed two days ago!" I cried. "You mean you were there all that time? Even at night?"

"I guess so," Shurik whispered. "I didn't want to go until I found her."

Tears welled up in my eyes. I hugged Shurik tightly.

"We'll look for her tomorrow. I promise. I'm sure that the firemen would know where she is."

The room began to smell of the delicious roasting potatoes. "Have you eaten anything during these two days?" I asked.

"Yes, I found an apple."

"And was that all?"

"Yes."

The water in my fire-blackened teapot began to boil and splatter on the coals. I pulled my mittens on and quickly drew the teapot out of the stove.

"In a few more minutes we'll have nice, hot tea. I even have a piece of sugar!" I said brightly.

Shurik's face, neck and hands were shiny with vaseline. They were finally clean of brick dust and grime. I combed his hair and lifted his pinched little face toward me. He was a beautiful child, blue-eyed and blond with thin, transparent skin. He sat shivering in front of the open stove, patiently waiting for me to give him something to eat.

I dug the black, cracked potatoes out of the coals. While they were cooling, I unlocked my jewelry case. Inside, wrapped carefully in a clean handkerchief, was a sizable lump of sugar. I had been saving it for New Year's Eve.

"Here," I said, "it's all for you!" I handed Shurik the sugar. He took it without enthusiasm. I felt disappointed. I had expected to see his face light up, but then I realized how sick he was. I touched his forehead. It was hot and dry. I felt his pulse. It was racing. He had a high fever. *I must get him to bed quickly,* I thought.

I poured hot tea into two cups and mashed Shurik's potatoes. I had no butter but lots of salt—plenty of coarse, grainy, dirty-looking salt. I remembered how, before the war, our janitor used to sprinkle the same kind of salt on the sidewalks during the winter to melt the snow. Now we were happy to eat it. How things had changed in a year!

Shurik ate his potatoes greedily.

Thank God, he still has an appetite. He can't be too sick then, I thought with relief.

We drank our tea and finished the potatoes. We used torn pages from the atlas as plates, for there was not enough water to spare for washing dishes. The glossy pages, wiped clean, could be used again until, finally, they would be good only for lighting the fire.

The room felt warm and cozy. I was drowsy with fatigue.

"Let's go to sleep. I'll fix the sofa for you. Take this aspirin."

I tucked him under a blanket on the sofa. For good measure, I put my coat over him. Then I blew the candle out. My own bed felt icy, but I knew that soon I wouldn't notice it. I would be fast asleep. Even the constant boom of the artillery barrage would not disturb me.

I awakened with a start. Shurik was restless. He tossed and thrashed about in bed, mumbling deliriously. I touched his forehead. It was still burning. Toward the morning, Shurik's fever seemed to subside. He opened his eyes and smiled faintly at me. I was glad that he recognized me and wasn't afraid.

"Listen, Shurik," I said seriously. "I must go to work now, but you stay here until I come back. You're ill, so you must stay in bed. We'll search for your mother as soon as you get better. Meanwhile, I'll ask whether the civil defense people know where your mother is. One thing you must realize: she is *not* at the bombed house. Perhaps she is in some hospital."

"No," Shurik said faintly. "She is not in the hospital. She is dead." I felt a chill run down my spine.

"Why do you say that?"

"I just know." There was resignation in his voice. It pained me to hear it.

"Nonsense!" I exclaimed. "Until we check the hospitals, we can't be sure of anything!"

"I just know," Shurik repeated and closed his eyes.

"Listen, Shurik, listen to my instructions. I'll light the stove now, so you won't be cold while I'm gone. Here is a slice of bread. Don't eat it all at once, even if you're very hungry. I'll cut it in three portions; eat only one piece at a time. One now, with tea; another, about noon; and the third when daylight begins to fade—about four-thirty or five. Soon after that I'll be home with more food."

Shurik nodded gravely.

I poured a cup of tea for Shurik and lifted him to a sitting position. *Too bad the sugar is gone,* I thought, as I held the cup to his lips. Shurik took two sips and fell back on the pillows. "I'll drink it later," he murmured. I stood there, watching him. He seemed to drift into sleep again. He was breathing evenly, his forehead glistening with perspiration.

I wish I didn't have to go, I thought, as I buckled my heavy automatic service pistol to my belt. Then, glancing at Shurik once again to make sure he was asleep, I left the room.

"Lieutenant Petrovskaya, you're five minutes late!" said the chief of the hospital as I hurriedly put my hospital attire over my military uniform. The pistol was in my way, but it was against regulations for an officer to be without his weapon even for a few hours.

"I'm sorry, Colonel Stern. I had an unexpected complication at home," I apologized. I had never been late before, and I hoped that Dr. Stern would be lenient.

He peered at me over his glasses. "What kind of complication?" The doctor was wiping his hands meticulously with rubbing alcohol, for even at the hospital we had to preserve water.

"Yesterday I found an orphan, a small boy, sick and alone. I took him in—at least until he is well." The chief looked at me owlishly over the gold rims of his glasses. His bushy eyebrows were drawn into one straight line over his old wrinkled face.

"I hope you know what you're doing. It is impossible for you to keep the child," he said, reading my inner thoughts.

"Oh, I know, Comrade Colonel, I know. But I won't keep him longer than necessary—a day or two at the most. Then I'll notify the civil defense authorities. They might want to evacuate him from the city."

"See that you do." He looked at me shrewdly. "I know it is hard, but you cannot keep him."

How did he guess that I would like to keep Shurik? My chief never ceased to surprise me with his astuteness.

I liked our chief. Dr. Stern had been in charge of the hospital from the very beginning of the war. He had been a professor of anatomy at Leningrad University, and despite his advanced age—he must have been at least seventy—he refused to be evacuated with the rest of the university staff. He chose to assume the arduous duties of chief surgeon at the newly established military hospital. It wasn't easy for Dr. Stern. For years he had been away from active practice, lecturing to generations of university students at the medical school, never actually treating patients. Now, in his old age, he had to assume responsibility for the lives of hundreds of wounded soldiers, relying on the help of half-trained nurses like myself. But Dr. Stern never complained. He knew that all younger doctors were in the armed forces and that all the best nurses were serving with the troops at the front. He realized that when the city was besieged, one had no choice but to do one's best with the available resources. That's why he never made us feel inadequate, though he must have suffered greatly from our lack of thorough nursing training. He knew very well that all of us became nurses, not because it was our chosen field, but rather because the necessities of war demanded that we serve our country in this way. He joked with us about it, making references to our real professions—teachers, actresses, dancers—and somehow, he made us feel that we were not too bad as nurses after all.

To supplement our all-too-short emergency course in nursing, Dr. Stern organized classes in anatomy, conducting them himself. It all meant that we had to remain at the hospital for an additional two hours each day, but no one complained. We all adored our Colonel Stern, who looked so unmilitary in his uniform that even his service pistol failed to look real. It had the appearance of an oversized toy.

Dr. Stern was, truly, the head, heart and soul of the hospital. He was everywhere. He possessed enormous vitality, so remarkable for a man of his age. He must have slept no more than six hours a day, never leaving the hospital for more than a brisk walk around the block. It was said that he had lost his entire family—his wife, his daughter and his three grandchildren—in one car accident just before the war. Now he was all alone, except for a son-in-law, who was a naval officer with the Baltic Fleet. Thus, the hospital, its personnel and its patients became the home and family for the distinguished professor.

I tied my white hospital smock at the back and hid my hair under a white cap. Then, washing my hands with alcohol, I followed Dr. Stern into the operating room.

It had been a big classroom before the war. Its three tall windows were decorated with intricate designs of frost crystals, glistening gaily in the bright winter sunshine. It was warm in this room, much warmer than in the wards or in the corridors. Dr. Stern insisted that the operating room always be warm. His old fingers refused to work in the cold.

There were six tables in the middle of the room, all occupied by patients. More were waiting on stretchers in the corridor outside.

Our day began. Dr. Stern moved from one table to another in assembly-line fashion, joking with the wounded here and there, talking to the nurses in a quiet, fatherly way. He addressed all of us by our Christian names, resorting to official military rank only to show disapproval, as he had with me this morning when I was late for work.

There were fifty patients with serious wounds this morning.

Thank God, no amputations, I thought, as I glanced at the big school blackboard which we used to write the schedules of our daily operations and treatments. There must have been a temporary lull at the front, for we were able to catch up with the flood of patients. For the first time in weeks no one was left on the trucks, and even the corridors were cleared of makeshift beds.

At noon we were finished. The second phase of our work at the hospital was about to begin—the treatment of the less seriously wounded in the wards.

Dr. Stern, surrounded by five operating-room nurses, and reinforced by the ward nurses, moved from bed to bed, prescribing medications, peering into the healing wounds or ordering changes of splints and casts. It must have been very difficult for our chief to reconcile himself to a primitive kind of care of the wounded. We had no X-ray equipment, nor even electricity. Casts had to be passed from one patient to another, with makeshift alterations each time. Splints were made from planks torn from school desks in the yard. But Dr. Stern kept reminding us that we were lucky to have a hospital at all, however primitive. "Any fool can work in a well equipped hospital," he would say. "But, comrades, try to heal the sick and the wounded in our environment; then you have something to be proud of. Think of field hospitals, quartered in tents, in this weather!" he kept reminding us all. "Think of the hardships of the field nurses. Then you'll appreciate what we have here." We all tried to do our best under the circumstances. Even the patients ceased to complain about their discomforts the moment Dr. Stern appeared.

After our work in the wards, we all went downstairs to admit new patients who were to arrive momentarily. Only ward-duty nurses were excused from working in admissions; they were needed in the wards, one nurse for every twenty patients.

It was always bedlam in the reception hall. We had several long tables lined up against the walls where receptionists wrote down administrative details about each patient. We, the nurses, were to provide first aid. When we had hot water, each patient was thoroughly washed, for everyone coming from the front was badly infested with lice.

Dr. Stern made a quick evaluation of each soldier's condition and gave orders for his placement in the wards.

Each convoy of wounded was accompanied by several field nurses—*druzhinnizi*—who wore automatic submachine guns negligently slung around their necks. Many times the girls had to use those guns to fight off enemy snipers who shot at them while they were trying to reach the wounded men. These tough *druzhinnizi* used to look at us, the hospital nurses, as if we were of a lower order. What did we know of *real* danger, the *real* war fought in the trenches? Had we ever seen a tank attack? Had we ever been shot at? To them, we were pampered city girls, well-educated and clever enough to escape *real* service by flaunting our college degrees. They all but accused us of cowardice.

But that was before the siege was tightened about the city. Lately the attitude of the *druzhinnizi* toward the hospital nurses began to change. Each time the rough front-line girls arrived in the city with their convoy of wounded soldiers, they saw the corpses lying in the streets, frozen in the snow. They knew they had been victims of starvation. The girls heard the never-ending bombardment and saw the devastation of one of the most beautiful cities in the world. Slowly they began to show signs of compassion and sympathy for those of us who had to remain at our posts in the stranded city. At the front at least there was plenty of food, while in the city all of us, young and old, were slowly starving to death.

The girls from the front began to show their friendship by sharing their own food rations with us. Each time they came to

Leningrad, they brought us cans of meat or fish, half-melted bars of chocolate which tasted like soap, lumps of gray sugar or a few raw potatoes. The sugar which I had given to Shurik was a gift from my front-line friend Valya.

She was a powerful peasant girl who could easily lift a grown man and carry him into the reception room. Valya once had seen me on the stage, just before the war. She recognized me now, in spite of my military uniform. It thrilled her that she knew a "real actress." She immediately became my friend. She worried about my sick pallor and loss of weight. I was sure that she committed a few acts of petty larceny to supply me with soap and sugar. I could give her nothing in return. I couldn't even invite her to stay with me during her trips to Leningrad. Valya had to return to the front immediately after her patients were admitted into the hospital. I felt embarrassed by accepting her gifts, but Valya only laughed.

"Don't worry," she hissed, for she suffered from perpetual laryngitis due to her constant exposure to inclement weather. "After the war I'll be going to your theater every night—free! You'll be giving me *contramarki,* free passes!"

Today, more than ever, I searched among the convoy's *druzhinnizi* for Valya's familiar face. Today I needed her gifts, for I had a sick, hungry boy waiting at home.

She wasn't there.

"Where is Valya Orlova?" I asked one of the *druzhinnizi.*

"She isn't here. She was wounded yesterday."

"Oh, no!" I cried. "Is she badly hurt?"

"Lucky for her—no. Just flesh wounds. Shrapnel. She'll be back in a week. They didn't even evacuate her. She is staying in our *zemlyanka,* our own foxhole. Say, aren't you Kyra Petrovskaya?" The *druzhinniza's* blue eyes widened in surprise.

"Yes, I am."

"I saw you in *Romeo and Juliet!* We saw the play last spring, with our high-school class!" she exclaimed excitedly.

I felt flattered. It seemed eons ago that I had played Juliet, but people still recognized me. Actually it had been only the previous May, a little over six months. But how much horror had come since then! Our country was at war, our people were in the midst of a deadly struggle for survival. My own mother dead—killed while digging trenches.

"Girls," yelled the blue-eyed *druzhinniza*, "look who I found! Kyra Petrovskaya, the actress who played Juliet!" I was immediately surrounded by an excited crowd.

Just like after a performance before the war! I thought. The same eager, smiling faces, the same friendly expressions of admiration. But now the girls were dressed in huge, grotesque sheepskin coats and felt boots instead of their best party dresses and dainty shoes. But the faces were the same—happy, young and excited.

"It seems that you all saw me play Juliet!" I joked.

"We did, we did!" they chattered in chorus. "Romeo and Juliet was a required play in our classics course at school!"

That explained it. Every week our company played a special matinee for the students of the Leningrad high schools, so, of course, they had all seen me on the stage!

"Where is Lieutenant Petrovskaya?" demanded someone in a loud voice. A large, powerful-looking older woman wearing the uniform of a captain came toward me.

I saluted. She wearily motioned with her hand as if brushing a fly away, instead of a crisp military salute.

"At ease. I have a parcel for you from Valya Orlova. She couldn't come. She was wounded, but she wanted you to have this." The captain, the commander of the company, handed me a small package.

"Thank you, Comrade Captain. How is Valya?" I asked anxiously.

"She'll be all right soon. Nothing serious," she said offhandedly. Then, looking at the girls gathered around me, she commanded them to return to the trucks. I barely had time to wave good-by to my new friends and to thank the captain for Valya's present before the trucks roared off to the front for a new load of wounded.

I had no time to look at Valya's package, but I knew it was food.

"Hurry, comrades, hurry!" I heard the voice of Dr. Stern as he entered the reception room. "Soon it will be too dark to process the patients. I have just been informed that we ran out of candles!" He swore mightily. Some of the girls giggled. It was so funny to hear our gentle, dignified doctor using truck drivers' expressions. Somehow, on his lips, Russian curses lacked conviction.

We worked fast. There was just about an hour of daylight left. If we didn't process all the newly arrived men, we would have to leave them on the stretchers until next day. Without the candles our entire night crew would have to work by the light of a few flashlights—not an easy task in a hospital crowded with more than 700 patients.

"Comrade Colonel?" I heard the faint voice of a man on a stretcher. I went to him.

"What do you want, soldier?" I asked gently, thinking that the man was in pain. "Can I help you?"

"I want to talk to the colonel," he insisted.

"The doctor will be with you shortly. But I can help you. I'm a nurse."

"It's not medical. I can wait my turn, but I have an idea."

"What kind of idea?" I thought that the soldier might be delirious. They often talked feverish nonsense while being processed.

"How to get you some candles, plenty of them." I was sure

that the man was delirious. How in the world was he going to get us candles!

To humor him, I said, "Well, tell me, and I'll submit your proposal to the colonel."

"We can make them." He saw that I didn't take his idea seriously. "I mean it. We can make them, right here at the hospital."

"But who has time to make candles, my friend? We have only three doctors and several nurses and a few more nurses who are off duty now."

"The patients, of course. There are plenty of fellows who are not seriously wounded, or who are recuperating. They will be glad to have something to do." I thought for a moment. His idea wasn't farfetched after all.

"What's your name, comrade?"

"Sergeant Nikolai Polivanov, sapper corps."

"Sergeant, I think you have something there. I'll call Colonel Stern."

I went to the doctor and waited until he finished examining a nasty leg wound.

"What did they do to you at the field hospital? Did they put cobwebs on your wound instead of medicine? It's so dirty!" The young lad tried to smile, but the pain must have been excruciating. A pitiful grimace spread across his face.

"Don't worry, boy, we'll fix you up. Here is a pretty nurse; she'll take care of you." Dr. Stern winked at the soldier and, turning to me, said, "Clean the wound thoroughly and pack it with a strip of gauze and antiseptic salve. Don't bandage it too tightly."

"Yes, doctor." He was about to move to the next patient when I caught his arm.

"Colonel, someone has a good idea about our candle problem.

He is right there on the stretcher." Dr. Stern peered at me quizzically, but said nothing. He knew that I wouldn't disturb him with mere nonsense. He went to Sergeant Polivanov.

I began to clean the wound of the young soldier. Once in a while I glanced at Dr. Stern. He was listening earnestly to Polivanov.

That night, Dr. Stern made a decision. Starting next morning, the hospital would go into mass production, making its own candles.

In the days to come the soldiers would respond eagerly to the idea of making candles from inedible fats and strips of old bandage. They were bored with the dull routine of the overcrowded wards. Doing something useful appealed to them. Sergeant Polivanov, the originator of the project, would not be among them. He was too badly wounded. In fact, he was one of our most serious cases.

Our work in the reception room was over. Soon our dour cook, Fyodor, appeared with two buckets of hot soup and a pile of sliced bread—our daily food ration. Only the doctors ate at a proper table, in the chief's office. Nurses usually ate at their stations.

Dr. Stern beckoned to me to follow him.

"Take your bread, but don't worry about soup. I'll have enough for both of us," he said.

I took a slice of bread from Fyodor, who checked my name on his list, indicating that I had received my daily ration. Then I followed the doctor into his office.

"Dear God, am I tired!" he said, stretching his arms and shaking his head. "There are days when I think that I won't live to see the morning. Today was one of them."

He looked old and worn-out.

"You should write to headquarters for an assistant," I volunteered. "You do everything yourself. You don't even have a day off!"

"You know that there are no more doctors available. Everyone is at the front lines. Sit down. I want to talk to you. But first, ladle us a bit of this slop, which Fyodor insists is soup!"

I filled two plates with steaming soup and served one of them to Dr. Stern.

"See if there's any meat on the bottom of the pot," he said. I stirred the soup and, indeed, there was a sizable chunk of meat, invisible in the muddy soup.

"Good!" Dr. Stern exclaimed with childish delight. "I don't care if it's horse meat or some old cow. It's still protein! Divide it in two and let's eat!"

I didn't waste time on unnecessary polite refusals.

"Now, tell me about your foundling," the doctor said, tucking a hospital towel under his chin in place of a napkin, ready to enjoy his dinner. "By the way, you may go home right after we eat. I'll excuse you for today from anatomy. Now, who is the boy?"

Leningrad in March 1941. Thousands of citizens clear the city of an accumulation of snow and debris. *Wide World Photos*

Young children in a shelter during an air raid. *Wide World Photos*

Army nurses among the ruins of the city in search of the wounded. *National Archives*

2

When I finally returned home and opened the padlock, I found Shurik asleep. The bread remained untouched, dried and shriveled now, but the tea was gone. I moved about the room, as quietly as possible, lighting the stove once more. I thought with dread of the necessity to trek to the river. It had to be done. I had no water left.

Shurik stirred, then opened his eyes. They were dull and vacant.

"Good evening, Shurik!" I said softly. "How do you feel?"

He looked at me for a few moments, as if not recognizing me. Then he attempted to smile.

"Awful," he said. "My bones hurt . . . and my head . . . and even my eyes," he said with effort.

I touched his forehead and took his pulse. He was still feverish.

"I brought you a real surprise," I said. "Just look at this!" I opened Valya's little parcel and brought its contents for Shurik to see. He glanced with indifference at our riches—two thick slices of smoked salami, one raw onion, two sections of a chocolate bar and a handful of broken hard candy.

"Look at all these sweets!" I exclaimed. But Shurik remained apathetic.

I sat next to him on the edge of the sofa. "Listen. I must go to the river now. Sleep until I get back. Then we'll have a little feast, all right?" He nodded, silently.

I hated to leave the room. The stove emitted wonderful warmth, the spicy smell of the salami was most enticing. *Maybe we can manage without water. Maybe there is enough snow on the window ledge outside which I might melt.* I opened the small window-pane used for ventilation and peered outside. No. There was nothing left. I had forgotten that only yesterday I had scraped all the fresh snow to make a cup of tea. No, I must go to the river. I dressed again, but instead of my military cap, I draped a thick woolen shawl over my head and shoulders, completely hiding my military insignia. I stuck my automatic pistol into the pocket of my overcoat; it was dangerous to walk to the river at night. It was rumored that there were bands of thieves who would murder anyone for a pair of good boots or a book of ration coupons. Usually I would not go to the river at night; even the thought of it sent shivers down my spine.

In the daytime it was different. There was safety in the numbers of people at the river. However, at this hour, there would be no one.

I looked at myself in the mirror. One would never think that I was a young girl. I was bundled up solidly, and only my nose was clearly visible under the folds of the shawl.

That's good, I thought. *No one will suspect that I'm in the service.* I had heard that there were bandits who attacked young military girls merely to obtain their guns. *Maybe I should leave my gun at home,* I thought. But I was reluctant to part with it. I felt safer carrying it.

Shurik was asleep again. In spite of his fever his skin was

pale and looked almost transparent. His closed eyelids were so thin that they looked blue. It was just twenty-four hours ago that I had seen him for the first time in my life, and already I was as concerned about him as if he were my brother. I pulled a child's sled from under my bed. It had a long rope attached to it, for I needed to secure my various containers by tying them individually to the sled. Trying to make no noise, I left the room, locking the padlock.

Going to the river with an empty sled was easy. I walked briskly in the middle of the unevenly frozen street, pulling my sled with its clanking pots and pans. There was no traffic. It seemed that it had been in some other life, on some other planet, that this wide thoroughfare had bustled with traffic. The streetcars used to clank deep into the wee hours of the night, the buses rattled and the automobiles honked at every intersection. No one was on the street now.

The whole city was dark. Not a ray of light shone from the windows, which were tightly curtained as protection against air raids. Even the blue emergency lights at intersections were out. The city had been without electricity for weeks.

Trudging along, I passed the wrecks of several streetcars and buses, solidly frozen into snowdrifts. They stood where the electrical power had failed them, or a shell had stopped them. They would have to remain there until the spring thaw.

The full moon shone brightly over the frozen Neva River. The Winter Palace, the former residence of the Russian czars, the Hermitage, Russia's most magnificent museum of art—all stood intact on the embankment, spared as if by a miracle from enemy bombs. I had heard that an artillery shell fell on the inner court of the palace; on the outside, however, the magnificent building appeared as serene as always.

There were several huge battleships immobilized in the ice

on the frozen Neva. Their antiaircraft batteries helped to protect
our city from air attacks, but their crews were small. Most of
the sailors were fighting alongside the foot soldiers at the front,
since the Baltic Sea had become infested with enemy ships. "Wait
till spring!" the wounded sailors at our hospitals used to say.
They felt ashamed that their ships had become inactivated and
that they, themselves, had to fight like "ordinary" soldiers. "Wait
till the ice melts! Then we'll go back to sea and show them what
Russian sailors can do!" Meanwhile, only skeleton crews remained on the huge, helpless ships.

I made my way cautiously down the slippery hill, only vaguely
resembling the sweeping, elegant wide staircase, which used to
lead to a pleasure-boat landing. If my sled weren't so loaded
with containers, I could have slid down the hill like a child. It
certainly would have been much safer.

Once on the ice, I made my way to the nearest *prorub,* a hole,
from which I would haul my water. I tied the rope to one of the
buckets and lowered it into the *prorub.* I heard a splash as the
bucket hit the water, and then I felt the rope tighten as it began
to fill up. As soon as I felt its full weight, I pulled it up.

With every new container to fill, it became more difficult. My
arms began to ache. I knew that more was splashing out than I was
pulling up.

Suddenly a narrow beam of light flashed into my face and a
loud voice, amplified by a bull horn, shouted, "Hey, you, there!
What are you doing?"

The light and the voice came from the silent navy ship.
Obviously the sailor on watch didn't trust me. He probably
thought that I was a saboteur, planting a mine to blow up his
cruiser.

"I'm just getting water," I shouted back. I hoped he wouldn't
start shooting at me.

The light beam jumped from me to my sled with its many
containers and then back to me.

"All right, *babushka*, take care not to fall into the *prorub!*" came the voice from the bull horn.

"Thank you, sonny, God bless you," I shouted back, smiling to myself that the sailor took me for an old grandmother—a *babushka*.

The trek back was laboriously tortuous. I could not pull my heavily laden sled up the slippery steps. I had to carry each container separately and, once on the street again, reassemble them on the sled, tying them one to another. Then, pulling the sled behind me, I turned toward home.

The empty wide street, silvery under the moon, lay ahead of me. I walked slowly, trying not to spill any more of my precious cargo, watching for deep ruts in the snow which could overturn my clumsy sled and make my trip to the river all for naught. The rope from the sled cut into my hand, even through my mittens. I had to change hands often to reduce the pain.

The last ordeal awaited me at home. I had to make several trips up and down the staircase, for I could carry only two containers at a time. With my last trip, I brought my sled up and stored it under the bed once again. I had enough water now to last for three days!

Shurik was still sleeping. The room was very warm. There was enough fire in the stove to begin the next phase in making the water potable. It was a tedious but necessary process. The water, drawn from the river, was polluted and needed to be boiled and strained twice before it was safe for drinking. Even after this it still had a muddy color, but at least it was no longer contaminated.

I thought of boiling just enough water for tomorrow morning. I was too tired. But the thought that Shurik might use the polluted water in my absence made me work until two in the morning, until the last container of water had been purified.

Shurik slept throughout the whole procedure. I thought of

awakening him and forcing him to eat, but I changed my mind.
Let him rest, I thought. *It's probably best for him now.*
I wasn't hungry either. Dr. Stern's generous portion of meat had
sated me. *It's all for the best,* I thought. *Soon it will be morning,
and we'll have Valya's salami for breakfast.* I undressed and went
to bed. I had only four hours to sleep. I could not waste even
one minute of it.

"How do you feel this morning?" I asked Shurik.
"I don't know . . . I feel very dizzy," he said in a hoarse
voice. Then his thin body shook with paroxysms of heavy, dry
painful coughs that left him exhausted. I supported his chest with
my hands, trying to reduce his pain. He looked at me, his eyes
slowly filling with tears.
"It hurts," he finally said, touching his chest. "It hurts all
over."
"I know, I know. I'll bring a doctor later, and he'll give you
something to make you better." Even as I said the words, I knew
I was foolish. There were no doctors to take care of the civilians.
But I continued to stroke him, murmuring encouraging words,
hoping that his coughing seizure would not return. He felt limp
in my arms. His body was so thin that it seemed I could feel his
every bone.
"Lie down, darling, keep warm. I must light the stove again."
Obediently Shurik fell back on his pillows. He watched me
as I prepared our breakfast, but his eyes were dull.
"Here we are. Breakfast is ready!" I announced cheerfully as
I spread a tablecloth on the little table in front of the sofa. I
didn't feel like eating off the *Great Soviet Atlas* this morning.
Valya's generous present required a more elaborate setting.
Shurik didn't stir.
"You must eat a little," I said. "You haven't eaten anything
for more than thirty-six hours or maybe longer. You're the world

champion of noneaters!" A slow smile spread across his thin face. He pulled his right arm from under the blanket and squeezed his hand into a fist.

"I'm the champion!" he declared hoarsely, holding his fist up, like a boxer.

He can't be too sick if he can still joke! I thought with relief.

I propped Shurik up with pillows. He looked like a pitiful little chick, his neck thin and long, his blond hair ruffled and moist. He drank his tea and sucked on a candy. I made him swallow a few bites of bread and salami, but I could see that he did it only to please me. It was time for me to leave. As I was buttoning my coat he beckoned me to come closer to him.

"What is it?"

"I love you," he said as his thin arms encircled my neck and his cracked, dry lips touched my cheek. "Please, don't send me to an orphanage."

"Don't worry. Rest now," I said, but I knew that I could not turn him over to the authorities. I didn't know how I was going to manage, but I was not going to send him away.

"Can you spare me one minute, Dr. Stern?" I asked as I knocked at the open door of his office.

"Come in," he said. "How is your foundling?"

"Oh, Dr. Stern, he is ill. He might even have pneumonia. He is so pitiful." In spite of my resolution to be brisk and professional, I began to cry.

"No, no, no. Don't do that. I can't stand women crying." Dr. Stern fussed over me, wiping my face with the skirt of his hospital coat. "I told you you should have taken him to the orphanage at once. Now it's too late, I know. You love him as if he were your own, no?"

I could only nod my head.

He walked to the window and stood there for a few seconds,

his back toward me. "I'll tell you what you must do. Since you chose to keep him, you must take the full responsibility for his welfare." He pointed his finger at me as if assigning me to this special duty. "Now I'll help you as much as I can. I'll split your shifts into two six-hour segments. It means, of course, that you'll have to come to the hospital twice a day, but you live nearby. Next, I'll make a personal visit to your——what's his name?"

"Shurik. Shurik Nikanorov."

"I'll see your Shurik, right after our morning treatments. I have a few medications here which we can spare."

"Thank you. Thank you, Dr. Stern!" I said, overcome by the way he had read my thoughts. He waived my thanks impatiently.

"This is all I need. A pediatrics case! I haven't seen a sick child in fifty years!" he grumbled, pretending anger. "What do you feed him?" he demanded.

"Tea, bread and salami."

"Tea, bread and salami," he mimicked. "What kind of a diet is that for a sick child?"

I began to cry again. "But I don't have anything else!"

"Stop. Stop crying at once!" He hurried to dry my tears. "We'll do something . . . I'll bring a bit of oatmeal and a can or two of condensed milk. We can't let the child starve just because it's against the regulations to take food out of the hospital. But stop crying, for God's sake!" He walked to the window again and stood there, examining the frost designs on the windowpane.

"Does he have fever?"

"Yes, doctor. He has high fever. For two days now. And he sweats. And he has a bad, hacking cough."

"I don't like it. You're probably right. He may have pneumonia. I'll see him today, I promise. Now run along. I must scrub for surgery." I left his office, feeling elated.

As I passed through the hospital wards, I saw that the patients were busy whittling with their pocketknives, fitting together the cumbersome forms for making candles. Sergeant Polivanov's idea had caught on. The initiator of this venture was our first surgical patient that day. He was stretched out on the operating table, both legs free of bandages, exposed for the doctor's examination and treatment. Even though I was a nurse I had to turn away. I had never seen such horribly mangled flesh.

Polivanov watched Dr. Stern anxiously.

"Can you save my legs, doctor?" he asked hoarsely.

"We'll try, sergeant, we'll try. Just relax, if you can, and close your eyes. Nurse, give Comrade Polivanov a good dose of morphine." Tonya, another surgical nurse, was ready with the injection. Deftly she administered the pain-allaying narcotic into him. Since the usual anesthetics were not available to us we relied heavily on morphine.

"Relax now. We'll be with you momentarily," said Dr. Stern, moving to the next patient.

I watched Polivanov's face. I liked him. He exuded strength and even now, lying helpless on the operating table, waiting for the morphine to take hold of him, he inspired compassion, rather than pity. He was big and ruggedly handsome and somewhat older than most of the soldiers.

I checked the equipment on my cart. Everything had to be ready for the long, exacting work ahead. I knew that here we had a two-hour operation, much longer than our usual average. After a few minutes I looked at him again. He was asleep. We worked on Polivanov for more than two hours. It was a miracle that he had any legs at all. The wounds were deep, and in some places his bones were shattered into many sharp splinters.

"He'll be lucky if he pulls through it without amputation or gangrene," murmured Dr. Stern behind his surgical mask.

"Will he be able to walk if he does pull through?" I asked.

"Yes, if he survives at all and if we manage to avoid amputation, he'll walk, but he'll have a bad limp," Dr. Stern said as he cleaned the last wounds, removing the splinters of bone and shrapnel, trimming away the torn flesh. There was a little mound of metal fragments on his table, to which he kept adding as he worked.

"Put all these pieces of shrapnel in a jar," he told one of the assisting nurses. "They like to see the thing which tore them apart. I have never seen a soldier yet who doesn't ask for the bullet that struck him."

"OK, lieutenant, he is all yours," Dr. Stern said to me. "Try to bandage his wounds separately so that if there is an infection in one it won't contaminate the other." He saw my hesitation and added, "If you look very closely, you'll see that it is possible to find tiny bridges where the bone and the flesh are still intact. Put plenty of antiseptic salve on, and do as I say." He turned to the next patient.

I asked an assistant nurse to bring me a jar of the sticky, smelly salve. I dipped long strips of gauze into the yellowish, oily substance and packed each wound, until every hole in Polivanov's legs was full of gauze. I covered each wound with still more gauze and salve. Over this I placed the widest bandages I could find.

When I was finished, the orderlies lifted Polivanov's limp body on a stretcher and wheeled him to the intensive-care ward. I changed my gloves and moved with the doctor to the next patient. And then to the next, and to the next. By one o'clock in the afternoon we completed surgery.

"Dr. Karpova," Dr. Stern addressed his young assistant, "please continue the ward treatments without me for the next hour or two. I must leave the hospital for a while."

"Yes, doctor. Any special orders?"

"No, my dear, just the routine. I'll be back for the staff meeting."

Captain Karpova had been one of Dr. Stern's students only six months ago. Everyone admired her, but few people *liked* her. She was only twenty-three and full of self-importance. She put a barrier between herself and the nurses, making it clear at every opportunity that she was a doctor and they, although of the same age, were to obey her. I was the only one of the "lower echelon" with whom she associated. Perhaps it was because she knew me as an actress. To me, she was a lovely young woman who happened to finish medical school in time to serve in the war. I obeyed her instructions—she surely knew more about medicine than I—but I refused to be overimpressed by her rank. This indifference to her status, plus her admiration for my own profession, made it possible for us to become friends. I liked her looks. She personified classical Russian beauty: tall, statuesque, with long, dark-blond hair which she braided to encircle her head like a coronet. She had perpetually rosy cheeks, which didn't fade even with lack of food and absence of fresh air and exercise. Like all of our doctors, Captain Karpova had to live at the hospital to be instantly available for any emergency.

Occasionally I saw her at the hospital in her off-duty hours. She looked young and fresh, with her hair hanging down her back in two thick braids, reaching well below her waist. She looked like a village girl. No one would have suspected she was a doctor of medicine. The wounded soldiers inevitably fell in love with her. But she sternly refused to acknowledge their admiring glances or their lovesick notes. Some people called her *snegoorochka,* the snow maiden, after the heroine of Russian folklore, who was a pure, aloof and cold beauty.

"Are you coming with me, lieutenant?" Dr. Stern asked me sharply from the door of his office.

"Yes, Comrade Colonel, immediately!"

Dr. Karpova raised her eyebrows.

"Are you going with the colonel? Where to?" She was ter-

ribly anxious to know everything that was going on in the
hospital.

"Don't worry!" I laughed. "It's nothing medical. Or, rather,
it is medical, but personal. I have a little orphan with me who
is sick. I'll tell you later." Dr. Karpova's beautiful face relaxed,
and she went into the wards, surrounded by a bevy of obedient
nurses. For an hour or two, she was to be in charge of the whole
hospital. I was sure that she felt very important.

The air was fresh and frosty. For the second day now we had
bright sunshine, so unusual in Leningrad during the winter. Dr.
Stern and I walked briskly toward my house. Our deep pockets
were bulging with canned milk, packages of oatmeal and even
a small sack of sugar. Dr. Stern forbade me to inquire where
he got the food.

"You'll be glad to know our rations may improve soon," Dr.
Stern said. "Apparently we now have a road right over the ice
of Lake Ladoga. We'll start getting more food supplies from the
mainland any day now."

The mainland! We, the blockaded, battered people of Leningrad, felt like isolated island dwellers, calling the rest of our
country "the mainland." It was a good description, for we were
surrounded by the enemy almost completely, except at Lake
Ladoga where there were three miles of shore line still in our
hands.

Now it seemed that through this narrow corridor we would
be able to receive help from the mainland and evacuate our
wounded to the safety of unoccupied territory.

"A road, over the ice?"

"Yes, that's what I heard," said Dr. Stern. "Of course, it can
be used only until the first thaw, but still . . . it has never been
done before." We walked in silence for a while, each thinking of
this great new and daring enterprise.

"They call it *Doroga Zhisni,* the Road of Life," continued

Dr. Stern. "I heard that there is a vicious battle going on right now for the possession of this road. If the enemy succeeds in closing it, God help us. We'll all be dead by spring." As if to underline these grim words, the air raid sirens began to whine.

"Here they come," I said to Dr. Stern as I heard the increasing drone of enemy bombers.

"Where?" The doctor squinted against the bright sun.

"Right over the House of Books. There are five of them. Let's hope that it's their one and only wave."

"They never come just in one wave. Right now they dominate our skies. There will be two or three waves, you'll see."

We heard the first dull thuds of the explosions in the direction of the river. The bombers were obviously after our stranded battleships. Soon the blue sky above us began to fill with dozens of gray puffs. Presently they turned into tiny white clouds as our antiaircraft batteries filled the skies with flak.

The second, then the third wave of enemy bombers appeared, but we didn't stay to watch. It was an everyday occurrence. We had grown used to it.

"Here is Shurik's house—or, rather what's left of it," I said as we passed the bombed building. Dr. Stern barely glanced at the house. His face was dark and sad. He was tired and sick at heart for his torn city.

"And here is my house. I live on the fourth floor. The stairs are steep, so let's preserve our strength." He gave me a sidelong glance.

"Are you implying that I'm old and decrepit? That I can't climb four flights of stairs without collapsing?" Then he smiled. "Well, you're right! I might collapse if we don't stop on every landing for a few moments. I have a bad heart." I wanted to say something sympathetic but Dr. Stern had already started up the stairs.

Shurik was awake. He smiled weakly and tried to sit up.

"Shurik, this is Dr. Stern. He would like to help you. He's a wonderful doctor," I said. I helped him take his coat off.

"Zdrastvooyte," Shurik said politely, extending his thin little hand in a grown-up manner.

"Zdrastvooi!" answered Dr. Stern, shaking Shurik's hand. "How are you feeling?"

"Not so good. I have pains all over."

"Well, we'll see what is wrong." Dr. Stern took a collapsible, old-fashioned listening tube from his pocket, adjusted it and pressed it to Shurik's chest. The tube was cold, and I could see Shurik's skin pucker in hundreds of tiny goose-pimples.

The doctor examined Shurik thoroughly, completely absorbed in what he was doing, paying no attention to my inquisitive glances.

When he was through, he turned to me with a broad smile.

"Get us some hot tea, woman!" he commanded, sounding like a rough peasant. Unexpectedly Shurik giggled.

"You said it just like grandpa used to say it to my grandma!" he said, still giggling.

"I am a grandpa!" declared Dr. Stern. "I have hundreds of grandchildren. All the children in the world are my grand-children!"

"I don't believe you!" Shurik challenged.

I was amazed. My Shurik was showing signs of life again!

"Doctor, you still didn't tell me what's wrong with him," I reminded my chief.

"Nothing's wrong. He just has a very nasty bronchitis. His lungs are clear. With good care, in a day or two he'll be as good as new. Let him stay in bed and feed him all the goodies that we brought with us. Here's some aspirin for him. Give him two tablets every four hours, and his fever will be gone by tomorrow. He is a strong, wiry lad; he won't stay sick much longer. Will you, Shurik?"

"No, doctor. I won't." Then a sudden fear flashed across his emaciated face. "But when I get better, you won't send me away, will you?" Shurik clutched the blanket with both hands, as if seeking protection against the fate which might dispatch him to the impersonal world of some unknown orphanage.

"No, darling, no! We won't send you away. I promise!" I cried and instantly wondered how I could keep such a promise.

Dr. Stern frowned. I knew that he disapproved of my action, but he said nothing. Shurik looked with uneasiness at Dr. Stern, but the chief pretended not to notice it.

"I'll make some tea," I said gaily, trying to ease the heavy uncertainty which hung in the air like a sticky fog.

"Doctor?" Shurik said timidly.

"Yes?"

"Can you promise, too, that you won't send me away?"

Dr. Stern shifted uneasily in the chair. He was on the spot, and he knew it.

"What do you mean?" he asked, stalling for time.

"I mean, will you send me to an orphanage when I get better? You're her commander, so if you order that I be sent away, she'll have to obey, even though she promised to keep me."

"I'll tell you the truth, Shurik," Dr. Stern said seriously. "According to our law we must send you to an orphanage."

Shurik's face, which only moments ago was bright with expectation, became sorrowful again. He closed his eyes wearily and once again became a listless, sick child.

"Then I don't want to get well," he whispered.

"What kind of talk is that?" Dr. Stern exploded with indignation. "You came to a wrong conclusion. You didn't let me finish. I said 'according to our law,' and it's true. But there are always exceptions. Are you listening to me, boy? Open your eyes!"

Obediently Shurik opened his huge blue eyes, which seemed to be sunk in their sockets, and looked directly at Dr. Stern.

"There are always exceptions," repeated Dr. Stern. "Furthermore, I believe that in this case we have a right to claim a genuine exception. You're not an orphan. You still have your father, and as far as we know, your mother might still be alive. So you're not an orphan. Why do you keep talking such nonsense? Who's insisting on sending you away?" In spite of his own better judgment, Dr. Stern found himself—just like I— promising to keep Shurik out of an orphanage.

"Then you do promise that you won't send me away?" insisted my charge.

"I promise."

Shurik smiled happily. Then he pulled himself to a sitting position and reached for a salami sandwich.

3

In a few days, just as Dr. Stern had predicted, Shurik's fever subsided. He was well on his way toward complete recovery. But he was faced with a new problem—boredom. There was nothing to keep him busy. No books. No games. All the stores, except a few food shops, were nailed shut with boards as a precaution against vandalism. Empty stores that commanded an unobscured view of the main city intersections had been converted into machine-gun emplacements. Their plate-glass windows had been replaced by brick walls, with only narrow slits left open for the protruding barrels of machine guns. They were manned by young women from light-artillery units who lived and slept next to their guns, ready to meet a possible invasion.

In our grim, fortified city there was no place to buy a box of crayons or children's books. But my good luck held. One morning our full-bearded old janitor ran into the nurses' room.

"Look what I've found," he cried excitedly. "It was inside one of the school desks we were about to chop up for firewood!" He handed me a box of colored pencils, with the name "Kolya Ivanov" written over the lid. "Give it to Shurik from me!"

I was amazed. I didn't realize that my involvement with Shurik was known to anyone but my closest friends at the hospital.

37

"Thank you, Vasily; this is exactly what I needed!" I took the gift. "But how did you know about Shurik?"

"Oh, everybody knows about him. Someone heard something about your finding an orphan who then told it to someone else. You know how it is. A hospital is like a small village; everybody knows what's cooking for dinner next door. However, give this to your lad too." He handed me one lemon drop wrapped in colored paper.

"Thank you, Vasily, I'll do that." The old janitor saluted me and smartly turned about-face as if he were an honor guard on parade and I were a general.

The first batch of our homemade candles was ready. We all awaited eagerly to examine the results of our unusual undertaking. Old Vasily, assisted by two kitchen girls, brought armloads of frozen candles from the yard.

"All right, light them up!" ordered Dr. Stern.

There were sounds of scratching matches. The candles were lighted. They sputtered and they hissed; their wicks, made of bandages, smoked and belched soot, and smelled of unpleasant, burning fat, but they burned, producing a dancing, uneven light. Shouts of victory filled the wards. Only the very ill and dying remained indifferent to our success. I took one of the lighted candles and went to check on the originator of our enterprise, Sergeant Polivanov.

Dr. Stern waged an all-out battle to save Polivanov's legs from amputation. The first step in this battle was to prevent the development of gangrene, which almost always under our primitive conditions led to amputation, and often death.

Dr. Stern didn't rely entirely on our scheduled examinations of the sergeant. He wanted to know more frequently if there were any changes in Polivanov's condition. We were instructed to smell the bandages every few hours. We gladly performed this unsavory task. Anything, in fact, was better than assisting at an amputation.

I sniffed the bandages. Thank God, nothing but the usual smell of salves and medications. One more day won for Polivanov. Placing the candle on the nurse's table, I took his temperature. It was very high, almost at the top of the thermometer's scale. In the journal of our daily medical procedures I made an entry opposite Polivanov's name, stating his temperature and the hour of my inspection. In the section reserved for special remarks, I wrote "no gangrenous odor" and signed it with my full military title. My day on duty was over. It was time to go home to Shurik.

The pale moonlight streamed into the room through a frost-covered window. I could barely see the outline of Shurik sitting on the sofa, huddled in a blanket.

"Cheer up, we'll have light in a moment," I cried as I cautiously made my way in the darkness to the table to unload the candles generously given to me by Dr. Stern. My own pre-war hoard of fancy dinner candles had become exhausted during Shurik's illness.

"What have you been doing?" I asked, knowing very well that his day must have been long and dull.

"Nothing. I was dreaming. And I slept a lot."

"Good," I said cheerfully. "In a minute we'll have a fire going and a candle lighted and"—I paused for dramatic effect—"I have a gift for you! Look what I brought. You can draw a picture while I light the stove." I handed the colored pencils to him.

He took the box and slowly opened it. I watched his face as a delighted smile spread across it.

"Oh, thank you! Where did you get them? Oh, I'm so happy!" He threw his arms around my waist and buried his face in the

rough fabric of my overcoat. His joy was complete and over-
whelming.

"Old Vasily, our janitor, found it inside one of the school
desks. He asked me to give it to you. And also—this." I gave
Shurik the lemon drop. He promptly put it into his pocket.

"I'll save it for later, when we have no sweets at all." Shurik
examined the pencils. "Look," he cried happily, "the burnt
sienna is brand-new."

"Yes, whoever this boy was, he must have just got his pencils,"
I said, searching for a piece of suitable paper for Shurik to draw
on. There was none. So I tore a blank first page from my
cherished edition of Shakespeare. Before long probably the book
itself would have to be burned to keep us warm.

"How do you know that it was a boy?" challenged Shurik.

"Just look on the lid. He wrote his name on it."

"Kolya Ivanov," Shurik read slowly. "I think I know him,"
he declared.

I laughed. "How can you? The name is very common."

Shurik didn't answer. He was busy drawing a picture of a
house with corkscrew smoke coming out of its chimney.

Dr. Stern paced the floor of his study in his usual preoccupied
way. I began to think that he had forgotten all about me. I was
standing at the door, waiting to be invited in. I cleared my throat
to remind him politely that it was he who had sent for me.

"Oh, yes, Comrade Lieutenant. Come in, come in, sit down
right here, at my desk." He fussed unnecessarily, moving a chair
for me from one side of the desk to the other. Obviously the chief
was disturbed. Whenever he was uneasy or angry, Dr. Stern made
a lot of useless movements to postpone an unpleasant confronta-
tion. He pulled at his long mustache, another sign of uneasiness,
and then faced me squarely. I had a sinking feeling in my

stomach. Something awful must have happened.

"I must tell you, lieutenant, that Shurik's mother was found dead. So legally he is eligible to be evacuated. Since he has no living relative except his father, who is at the front, this makes him a ward of the city."

"But we promised——"

"I know," sadly agreed Dr. Stern. "It was very foolish of us. But we can't let this promise of ours prevent us from doing the right thing. He must be evacuated. Think of the danger of living in a blockaded city, of the bombing, of the epidemics which are sure to come in the spring. The boy should be going to school. Instead, you keep him in your room under lock and key. No, we must send him to a children's center for later evacuation. It's the only proper thing to do," he concluded.

"I suppose you are right," I finally said. "It is the only thing to do. But how are we going to explain it to him—after all our promises?"

Dr. Stern sucked on his mustache in silence.

"I don't know," he said at last. "You must think of something. I must admit I'm a terrible coward, and I won't face this dilemma. You"—he pointed his finger at me—"you must do it somehow. And the sooner the better. Tonight." He stood up behind his desk looking embarrassed. "It's for his own good that we must do it. Remember that."

"Yes, colonel."

"Do it tonight!" he repeated and dismissed me with a sigh of relief.

I felt wretched. I finished my work and, without talking to anyone, hurried home. It was snowing again. The few bright sunny days of winter were over. We were back to the usual icy winds from the Arctic, which blew the stinging snow about, making the city appear ghostly and foreboding in the constant twilight. Before the war we had bright street lamps lighted as early as 3:00 P.M. to disperse the gloom of the winter day. The snow would dance around the lighted globes of the lamps, and the streets somehow looked mysterious, even beautiful, but never foreboding, in spite of the huge drifts of snow and penetrating wind.

But that was before the war.

Now every drift of snow might be covering the dead. Every dark alley might be hiding someone ready to murder in order to take possession of a ration card or a pitiful half-pound of bread.

As usual, I walked in the middle of the street. It was safer there, for whoever might be hiding in the alleys or doorways would have to leave his stalking place to get to me. It would rob him of the element of surprise and give me a chance to draw my gun. Besides, walking in the middle of the road protected me from the garbage and slops. The citizens, weakened by starvation, often were too sick to walk down the stairs to the refuse dumps set up in every courtyard. Instead, they dumped their garbage and excrement out their windows. The façades of the apartment buildings were marred by long streaks of slops, frozen to their surfaces. I shuddered when I thought of the spring thaw. What a stench would hang over the city!

I opened the door of my room. Shurik was standing facing the wall but quickly turned toward me. There was a guilty expression on his face, and he smiled timidly.

"I didn't mean to mess up your wall," he began quickly. "I was trying to wash it off, but it won't come off."

He pointed to the wall. "I was just tracing the design on the wallpaper in this corner with my pencils. And somehow"—he spread his arms as if to encompass the whole room.

I lifted the candle and inspected the damage. The whole corner of the room was covered with many colored scribbles. Hot anger welled up in me. My beautiful new wallpaper!

I felt like striking the child who stood before me, a wet sponge in his hands and a frightened look on his face. He tried to wash the mess from the wall. Instead he made it even worse. The embossed parts of the wallpaper disintegrated from the application of water, while the garish colors of the pencils became anything but brighter.

"Why did you do it?" I shouted, unable to control my anger.

"I . . . I . . . I didn't have any paper. I didn't mean to. I just wanted to color a little . . . right here, in the corner, behind the bookcase. I thought no one would ever see it. But somehow I began to color higher and higher. And then, before I knew it, I was almost at the window. I'm sorry!" He sobbed, afraid to come near me.

The sight of his tear-streaked face, his scared eyes, had a calming effect on me.

What the devil, I thought, *it's just wallpaper. We're lucky to have a place to live in. And here I am, angry because of the ruined wallpaper.* Shurik watched me through his tears.

"Come here," I said. "Help me light the stove."

"You're not angry?" he asked cautiously.

"No. But promise never to do it again."

"I promise!" he cried happily, rushing to me like an exuberant puppy. "I love you so!"

I had pangs of pain in my heart. How could I tell him now about sending him to an orphanage? Surely he would think that I was punishing him for messing up my wall. No, I couldn't do it. Let Dr. Stern do it himself. Let him tell it to Shurik.

"I love you, too, Shurik," I said tenderly. "Let's forget about the wall. When the war is over, we will repaper this room with even more beautiful wallpaper."

"I wish it were over now," he sighed, preparing to go to bed.

"So do I," I answered absent-mindedly, wondering how I could bring Dr. Stern to meet with Shurik after he confessed his inability to face the problem.

At ten o'clock I had to return to the hospital to begin the night shift. I looked at the sleeping Shurik, covered him with another blanket and, locking the door securely with a padlock, left the room.

I came back home at eight o'clock in the morning. Shurik was just waking up.

"I had a good dream last night," he said, his face looking rosy after his sleep. "I dreamt about animals. I was in the zoo."

"It must have been a lovely dream," I said, smiling.

"It was." He stretched and lay quietly, thinking of his dream.

"I've heard from some people at our old house that all the animals at the city zoo were shot and sold for meat. Even snakes."

"What nonsense," I retorted. "I'm sure that our government evacuated the animals to some faraway city, like they did with the art treasures from the Hermitage."

"But some of them could have been eaten just the same," stubbornly insisted Shurik.

"I'll tell you what. Draw a picture of the zoo for me. But not on the wall," I added hastily.

"This afternoon I'll take you with me to the hospital to see Dr. Stern," I continued, thinking, *Let the colonel deal with Shurik's destiny.*

We had a meager breakfast. While I went to the river for our water supply, Shurik busied himself with his picture of the zoo.

It was a formidable drawing. On one page from my Shakespeare, Shurik drew an entire zoo. He didn't miss a single exotic animal. There were lions and tigers, elephants and monkeys, giraffes and crocodiles. It was a beautiful picture. I had never seen a drawing by a ten-year-old done with such accuracy as to color and shape of its subjects. The only thing, which struck me as strange, was the absence of cages. The animals in Shurik's picture intermingled peacefully behind a gate with a sign LENINGRAD ZOO. There were a few figures of people with colorful balloons. Every available space was filled with drawings of daisies or bluebells.

"It's beautiful, Shurik," I said, examining his picture. "But I don't see any bars or cages in your picture. Aren't you afraid that all these wild animals might eat one another and the people, too?"

"No," he said seriously. "After the war I'm going to invent a special pill which the zoo keepers will feed to the animals to make them friendly. Then we all can walk in the zoo and pet the tigers or hippopotamuses. Everybody will be friendly and kind. Even cobras will be gentle. Then we won't need cages. Only the wall around the zoo, so that the animals won't run away and be killed by a streetcar."

I looked at my imaginative child and thought stubbornly, *I won't let them take him away. I won't!*

The hospital was full of newly arrived wounded from the Tikhvin section of the front. The empty convoy of ambulances was just pulling away as Shurik and I entered the reception room. I caught a glimpse of my friend Valya, who was back after several days in the field hospital. Her arm was still in a sling but obviously it didn't prevent her from going on convoy duty again.

Shurik observed with interest the goings on in the reception room. He sat quietly on a designated chair in the corner, waiting patiently for me to take him to see Dr. Stern, who was still in the operating room. A nurses' aide, a girl of no more than fifteen, came to fetch me.

"Dr. Stern wants you in the operating room," she announced.

"Nurse Andreyeva fainted during the amputation and the doctor needs another nurse. Hurry!"

"Whose amputation? Polivanov?" I queried, dreading her answer.

"No, no, Sergeant Polivanov is still all right. I mean, it's not he."

"Fine, let's go." I turned to Shurik. "Wait for me. I must go to the operating room now. I hope it won't be too long, but you stay right here. Do you understand?"

"Yes," he said obediently.

The young girl helped me to change into my operating gown and poured alcohol on my arms and hands.

"Is he your brother?" she asked. "He looks just like you."

"No. He is my son," I said. I didn't know what made me say such a silly thing. The girl gave me a quick look. She obviously made some mental calculations and concluded that I must have had a child at the age of eight or nine.

"Where is Lieutenant Petrovskaya?" bellowed Dr. Stern from behind the closed door.

"Here I am, Comrade Colonel. I couldn't get here sooner, I was scrubbing."

"Well, take your place and finish bandaging this arm," he said, indicating the stump of an arm of a soldier, still on the operating table.

The routine of the work made me forget about Shurik. Suddenly Dr. Stern asked me through his mask, "Well, how did it go with Shurik?"

I was bandaging my last patient, and I hesitated with my answer.

"I couldn't do it, doctor. I brought him here," I confessed. "You tell it to him. And then punish me, if you wish. Court-martial me, if you wish, but I can't do it!"

Dr. Stern was silent. He finished his work, waited for the nurses' aides to wheel the last patient out of the room, and then he faced me.

"I thought that you wouldn't be able to do it. I even thought of sending a representative of the children's home to your house in your absence to take Shurik away, but I, too, couldn't do it. Let's go downstairs and meet the problem together."

My heart sank. I still hoped that somehow I would be able to convince Dr. Stern not to insist that it would be better for Shurik to be taken from me. I thought that I could suggest to him that, at the present, there were no evacuations from the city and, while waiting for one, Shurik might as well live with me. But the colonel was already descending the stairs leading to the reception room and opening the double-glass doors.

Suddenly he stopped at the door, peering through it. Silently he motioned me to join him and look inside. In the reception room, with stretchers of moaning soldiers, Shurik was moving from one man to another. In his hand he held a pitcher and a tin cup. He was avidly pouring water for the thirsty, feverish wounded. With some he helped raise their heads; with others he patiently trickled water right into their open mouths.

"Just watch that boy!" whispered Dr. Stern with admiration. "He is like an angel of mercy!"

We watched Shurik for a long time. He walked among the wounded men as if he were a grown man, a doctor, or at least a kind male nurse. He was talking to them, for we could see his lips move, and we saw smiles on the faces of the suffering soldiers.

"Colonel, please, listen to me!" I whispered, suddenly inspired by a new idea. "Please let Shurik stay with me and work at the hospital! He can do thousands of things, run errands, help as he is doing now; he can work in the kitchen." I talked fast, for I felt that it was a propitious moment to reach the heart of my kind chief. "Look how good he is," I continued. "Not one of our nurses' aides in sight and yet, look how well he manages! There is no evacuation of civilians right now. At least allow him to stay with me until evacuations resume. Please!"

The colonel opened the door. "What are you doing, Shurik?" he asked sternly.

"I am just helping. They asked for water, and I gave it to them."

"Don't scold him, Comrade Colonel," said one of the wounded. "The lad was a real help to us."

"Lieutenant, bring Shurik to my office," ordered Dr. Stern. "And write for me the names of the nurses' aides who are supposed to be on duty at the reception room."

"Yes, Comrade Colonel." I saluted.

Shurik looked at me in alarm. "Did I do something wrong?" he whispered.

"No. No, my darling, you did just fine!" I said happily, for I noticed a hint of a smile on Dr. Stern's face when he ordered me to bring Shurik into his office.

We all ascended the stairs without talking. Shurik kept glancing at my face, trying to read what was going on, feeling instinctively that it had something to do with him. I hoped devoutly that I understood Dr. Stern's smile correctly and that he indeed had a change of heart concerning Shurik's future.

"You did a fine job, Shurik, down there in the reception room," finally said Dr. Stern, almost at the door of his office. "Would you like to work at the hospital everyday?"

Shurik looked at him askance. "Do you mean it, honestly?" he asked suspiciously.

"Honestly!" Dr. Stern pressed his hand to his heart and then saluted. *"Tchestnoye Pionerskoye!—*upon Pioneers' honor!"— using the traditional saying of Russian Boy Scouts.

"And I can continue to live with Kyra?" Shurik demanded in a bargaining tone.

Dr. Stern faltered. He glanced at me. Then he said, nonchalantly, as if there had never been any discussion about Shurik's removal to the children's home, "Why, of course you can still live with her." I almost laughed, but I said nothing. My old foxy chief! He had many surprises.

"Then I accept your offer," Shurik said magnanimously. "What will I have to do?"

4

I hurried to the office of supplies to find a suitable uniform for Shurik. Ozerov, our *Zavkhoz* or director of supplies, was sitting behind his desk, watching two orderlies count linen on the floor. He was fat and very short. His head was always clean-shaven, and it gleamed like a polished billiard ball. He had enormous, protruding ears which looked like the wings of an exotic butterfly, for whenever he stood against the light, his ears appeared to be almost transparent, pink at the edges and deep-red closer to his head. He had the puffy face and pasty complexion of one who never exercised, and who rarely ventured out of the confines of the building.

He never talked. He barked orders instead. He spoke in a crisp, stàccato voice, delivering sentences shorn of all niceties, leaving only the bare, essential words. In his parlance, expressions like "thank you" or "may I" didn't exist. He liked to be saluted, and he insisted that the recuperating soldiers stand at attention when he entered the wards.

"What do you want?" the *zavkhoz* asked me with irritation. He didn't like me. But then, he didn't like anyone.

"I need the smallest white gown, to fit a person about this high." I put my hand at chest height.

50

"What have you there? A midget?" he sneered.

"No. A child," I said evenly, ignoring his contemptuous tone.

"It's a military hospital!" he declared, as if I didn't know. "No children allowed."

"This child is an exception. He'll be working here. By order of Colonel Stern," I added. Ozerov snorted.

"I have no small gowns," he said rudely, hoping undoubtedly to intimidate me.

"Yes, you have," I insisted politely. "I know that you have some short gowns. All the girls wear them. May I have one immediately? The colonel is waiting."

Ozerov knew that it was useless to argue. He rang a bell, and I observed him giving orders reluctantly to bring one short gown to Dr. Stern's office.

"You'll be responsible for this item. No alterations—it's government property. Dismissed!" He saluted me and sat down at his desk again, pretending to be busy with his papers.

I looked at him with open amusement. He dismissed me! What nerve! I couldn't let him get away with it. Instead of leaving, I said with malicious innocence, "By the way, I've heard that you won't be with us anymore. I've heard that you have volunteered to go to the front lines. What a noble thing to do." I heard no such thing, but I just couldn't help myself. I had to shatter his hostile pomposity somehow and, if anything, to pay him back for acting so grandiose toward his fellow workers at the hospital.

He blanched. I could see that he almost said that he never volunteered for anything, but he thought better of it and said nothing. I waved to him unmilitarily and left his office at a leisurely civilian pace. *A coward and a small despot within the confines of his department of supplies,* I thought, happy that I needled him.

In Dr. Stern's office we dressed Shurik in his new hospital uniform. The gown, the smallest one to be found, was still too big for him. We rolled his sleeves up and encircled his waist with a belt, but the gown still trailed on the floor behind him.

"He'll trip over the hem. He can't wear it this way. You must shorten it," said Dr. Stern, looking over the funny little figure of Shurik, all but hidden by the white gown.

Only the tips of his *valenki*, his felt boots, were visible beneath the folds of the garment.

"Lieutenant Ozerov says that we're not to tamper with government property, or we'll be prosecuted."

"Nonsense!" the doctor snorted contemptuously. "Here,"— he handed me a pair of large scissors from his desk—"cut it at the proper length and then hem it. The same with the sleeves."

Gladly I kneeled at Shurik's feet and cut away a sizable length of cloth.

"Do the same with two more gowns. I think three will be sufficient for Shurik." The colonel went behind his desk to write a memo.

"I'm requesting two more gowns for Shurik over my signature. I don't think that our zealous *zavkhoz* would care to prosecute me for 'tampering with government property.' " He peered at us over the rim of his glasses in his usual owlish manner.

"Now, you two run along, and tomorrow I'll expect Shurik to start working. OK?"

"OK, Comrade Doctor," Shurik said seriously, adopting Dr. Stern's Americanism without any difficulty. He shook the colonel's hand like a grown man as we left the office.

The next few days were very hard on me. A fierce battle was taking place on the approaches to Leningrad, tripling our load of wounded. All of us were on extra duty. With my best intentions toward Shurik, I could do no more than see him now and then as he hurried efficiently along the corridors on some errand. But Shurik did fine. I didn't have to be concerned about him. During this extraordinary emergency, Dr. Stern ordered a cot for his office, where Shurik slept. The rest of us caught cat naps at our stations, or on heaps of dirty laundry, or wherever we could find an empty space, for all the beds and stretchers were occupied by the wounded.

A vicious battle raged for possession of Tikhvin. Only a month ago the Germans took this little town, cutting Leningrad off from the rest of the country. If we were to survive, Tikhvin had to be retaken. The soldiers—most of them Leningraders—knew that the city would slowly starve to death if they did not recapture this last remaining railroad link with the mainland.

We in the city knew that the situation at the front must have grown worse, for our rations were cut again. At the end of November our daily ration of bread was only nine ounces for working men and four and a half ounces for dependents and children. There was practically nothing else.

Then, on December the eighth, the public address radio interrupted its scheduled program of poetry readings. On every street corner small groups of emaciated people gathered, listening to the announcement, forgetting momentarily their gnawing hunger. They were listening to the radio with new hope glimmering in their eyes.

"*Govorit Leningrad*—Leningrad speaking, Leningrad speaking"—the sonorous voice of the announcer was saying again and again. "Our glorious troops under the command of Generals Meretzkov and Khozin took Tikhvin. Tikhvin is in our hands! The end of the blockade is in sight! Our cause is just. We'll be victorious!"

That night we had another piece of exciting news—America had been attacked by Japan! Selfishly we didn't think of the devastation of the American fleet at Pearl Harbor. To us, the only important thing was that America, with its men and industrial might, was our ally now.

We celebrated this double event at a staff meeting in Dr. Stern's office. The colonel unlocked his safe and brought out a bottle of vodka.

"Comrades, let's drink a toast to victory," he said, lifting his glass.

"To victory," we shouted, raising our tin cups and swallowing the fiery liquid in one gulp.

"Please sit down, comrades, and let our commissar, Comrade Churakov, give us the news and the orientation report." We took our places around the room. Only a skeleton crew remained on the wards to take care of emergencies. Everyone was anxious to hear the news.

The commissar, a giant of a man in his early forties, was a navy man, badly wounded during the evacuation of Tallinn. He spent several months in a naval hospital where they fought valiantly to save his leg, but in vain. It was amputated above the knee. Commissar Churakov refused to be demobilized. The headquarters assigned him to Leningrad, to our hospital. He hobbled around on one leg with the help of a crutch, knowing very well that it would be a long time before he could get an artificial limb. Only food and war supplies were delivered to the city over the ice of Lake Ladoga.

He was a handsome man, and I couldn't help thinking that it was a pity that such a fine, intelligent man had been maimed for life, while our fat "zavkhoz," conceited and obnoxious, was safe and well off.

"Comrades," began Commissar Churakov, "you've heard that Tikhvin is back in our hands. If you look at this map, you'll see how important this little town is for the survival of our city."

He unfurled a school map of Leningrad and its environs and hung it on the wall. Using a pencil as a pointer, he indicated a small circle on the Leningrad-Vologda railroad line. It was Tikhvin.

"As you can see, all other rail lines linking us with the mainland are in enemy hands. With the loss of Tikhvin last month, we were almost doomed." He hesitated, as if he had said too much. It wasn't popular to admit publicly the desperate situation of our encirclement.

"Although we have built a railroad twenty kilometers long from Lake Ladoga to Zaborye, around Tikhvin, it was too close to the enemy. Only half of the freight was ever able to reach the city. Now, with Tikhvin again in our hands, we can bring freight directly to Leningrad, as soon as we rebuild the bridge over the Volkhov River." He pointed to the map again.

"Here, on our side of the lake, we are creating a port at Osinovetz. From this port we will be able to evacuate our wounded as well as those who are not essential to the defense of our city. Convoys from the mainland with food and materiel will arrive at this same port, too." He shifted his weight from his leg to the cane. I could see that his arm trembled, and his hand, clutching the cane, turned white at the knuckles. The commissar wasn't used to his crutches yet.

"I have a request from the commander of the Leningrad front that more medical personnel is needed at Lake Ladoga. Our hospital is to send five nurses and one doctor to the new front at the lake. The tour of duty will be extremely hazardous, so we'll rotate our personnel every two weeks. Is that clear?"

We all nodded.

"I have a list here. These comrades are to report to me personally tomorrow morning at seven o'clock."

He began to read his list. Dr. Karpova and I were among the first group to be sent to the new front.

5

On the morning of December the ninth, we started on our way toward the Road of Life. We were issued warm sheepskin coats and cotton-padded pants and jackets. We wore two pairs of coarse woolen socks and *valenki*. Our heads were protected by *shapka-oushánka*—fur caps with ear flaps—and we wore heavy woolen mittens. Thus, we were well equipped for the Arctic cold of the lake region, where temperatures often fell 30° and 40° below zero.

The sheepskin coats had a very unpleasant odor, as if "the sheep were still wearing them," as one of our nurses quipped, but we knew that this was far preferable to freezing in the icy winds.

We boarded an old bus. It was operated by burning wood in a fantastic contraption which was attached to its rear. It looked like a homemade stove, and it emitted dark puffs of smoke through its long tin chimney.

It was full daylight when we finally left the city after being joined by the personnel from other hospitals. We all knew the seriousness of our assignment. Now we waited for someone in charge to outline our duties and to describe the general situation awaiting us at the lake.

"Your attention, comrades." I heard a rasping feminine voice. "I am your commissar, Captain Teleghina." I looked up. Captain Teleghina was indistinguishable from the rest of us, for she wore the same kind of garb, had the same thin face and hoarse voice, resulting from perpetual cold.

"First, I want to call the roll. Then, I'll give you the latest news from the Ladoga front."

She read our names, and we answered, "present," like school children. She studied the face of each answering person for several seconds, as if to imprint it on her memory.

"Here are the facts," continued the commissar. "As you all know, we can trace the beginning of the blockade of Leningrad to our loss of Mga, last August. That railroad center was our last direct link with the mainland."

I shuddered. I hadn't known that our fate had been sealed as early as August. Just at the time when my mother died, digging antitank trenches on the approaches to Leningrad. Killed by a strafing enemy plane. I closed my eyes. The pain of the memory was unbearable. I tried to concentrate on what the commissar was saying.

"After the fall of Mga we had no way of bringing supplies into the city or to evacuate our wounded. The railroad to Moscow was cut by the Germans, as well as the road to Vitebsk. As you know, there are bloody battles raging right now around those cities.

"I don't want to scare you, but the situation on all fronts is very critical, most of all on our Leningrad front. We have three million people trapped in the city. I don't need to tell you how they are suffering. You all are part of these three million, and you all know personally what it means at this time to be a citizen of Leningrad.

"You remember, of course, the eighth of September. It was the day the Germans began to bomb us from the air. That was the night our Badayevsky warehouses burned. That was the night our food supplies went up in flames."

"And starvation began," said someone.

"Yes, and starvation began," the commissar agreed. "But bad as it was, we still held the Vologda Railroad, farther east, at Tikhvin. A trickle of supplies still could be brought into the city by a roundabout route, through Tikhvin. Then, in November, we lost Tikhvin. Now the Germans were only a few kilometers away from the armies of their allies, the Finns, who were occupying the Karelian Isthmus approaches to Leningrad. We couldn't let our enemy forces link their strength against us. So we counterattacked and, as you know, yesterday we retook Tikhvin."

We all began to smile, despite the seriousness of her orientation report. Even the commissar's thin, weather-beaten face cracked into a smile.

"My husband was killed at Tikhvin," she continued, serious again. "So, returning there now means a lot to me. Anyhow, your duty at Lake Ladoga will be to reinforce the existing medical staff which was badly depleted during the battle. The enemy undoubtedly will try to regroup and retake Tikhvin. There will be many casualties."

"What are the working conditions at the lake?" asked one of the doctors. "Are there any hospitals?"

"None. The countryside has been leveled. We'll have only tents or ice huts to live in and to work in. Later on, I'm sure temporary wooden structures will be built and the hospitals within the towns and villages repaired or rebuilt. But it will be later, when Tikhvin is securely in our hands. But now—today, tomorrow, or next week—we'll have tents or ice huts."

"What about our medical supplies? Instruments, medications?" asked another.

"Primitive. But I think that in a few days supplies from the

GERMAN INVASION 1941 — BLOCKADE OF LENINGRAD

Finnish Forces

German Forces

to Murmansk

to Moscow

to Vologda and Ural Mts.

LAKE LADOGA

GULF OF FINLAND

LENINGRAD

Kabona

Lavrovo

Voibokalo

Osinovets

Ice Road

Iushkelovo

Beloostrov

Kronstadt

Peterhof

Pulkovo

Pushkin

Neva R.

Tosna R.

Tosno

mi.

0 5 10 15

N

MAP BY RONALD WAYNE

mainland will be delivered. Remember, the railroad from Tikhvin goes all the way through Vologda and on to the Urals, to Siberia. We'll get our supplies."

It was a pleasant, comfortable feeling to know that once again we were connected with the rest of our country, even if only by a thin, frail thread.

"Our main base will be in Osinovetz, on the west bank of Lake Ladoga," continued Teleghina. "It is only about fifty kilometers from Leningrad, and we have a suburban railroad linking it to the city. However, our main work will be on the ice, clear across the lake up to Lednevo and Novaya Ladoga."

"I thought that we were going to Tikhvin," murmured Dr. Karpova, obviously disappointed.

"There is still fighting around Tikhvin. We are needed on the supply route," dryly commented the commissar, who overheard the remark.

We entered the forest and it became very dark. I could hear the engines of other vehicles as they passed us from the opposite direction. I closed my eyes and inched closer to Dr. Karpova's side for a bit of warmth.

We stopped with a jolt, and I woke up. A stream of cold wind rushed into the bus as someone opened the door. It was already twilight.

"Everybody out," shouted the commissar. "This is Osinovetz, our destination."

With great effort I stood up. My body ached from several hours of sitting on the floor. The cold made me feel numb.

"We'll have a hot meal in a few moments at headquarters!" promised Captain Teleghina.

Like nothing else, the prospect of a hot meal made us leap out of the bus. We had had nothing to eat since our departure from Leningrad, where we had a cup of hot tea and a slice of bread. For some reason no one thought of providing us with dry rations. We never expected that the usual trip of two or three hours would stretch into more than seven. I stepped out of the bus onto hard-packed snow and looked around.

In the gathering darkness of the evening I could see several low wooden barracks and a cluster of peasants' huts. A few yards away was the forest from which we came. The roadway disappeared under the trees. A convoy of trucks was entering the forest, moving slowly in low gear, traveling without lights, rolling toward Leningrad.

In the opposite direction I could see an immense stretch of snow, looking gray in the twilight and disappearing on the horizon, which I knew was there, but which I could not see. The dark-gray sky and the snow formed one endless void. It was the frozen expanse of Lake Ladoga, the largest in Europe. I remembered reading somewhere that Ladoga was thirty-one times as large as Lake Geneva in Switzerland. It was more than 125 miles long and, in some places, it was over 80 miles wide.

There were many uninhabited rocky islands in the lake, covered with dense woods. The lake was very deep, and part of an intricate system of canals linking the White Sea with the Baltic.

"This way, comrades," I heard the voice of our commissar.

There were no lights anywhere. The dark figures of people moved as if sleepwalking, with arms outstretched like blind men, often colliding with one another. We followed our commissar in single file. She led us toward one of the low-built barracks.

"We'll eat and sleep here. It's too late to proceed. Pass the word along the line," she said over her shoulder.

There was light inside the building, provided by two large kerosene lamps standing at each end of a long table made of plain boards. The flickering light of the lamps threw grotesque shadows on the log walls, making us all appear to be ten feet tall.

Half a dozen tired, unshaven Red Army men, the drivers of convoys, sat around the table. Some were asleep, their heads propped on their arms. Others were eating soup from tin bowls, which looked more like dog dishes than utensils for human beings.

But it was warm. Even hot, for there were two woodburning stoves at opposite ends of the long building, both crackling with a jolly fire, sending waves of warm air to unthaw our frozen limbs.

"Make yourselves comfortable, comrades. There are latrines behind the building. Women on the left. Men on the right," said our commissar. "If we're lucky, we might find a barrel of water at the entrance . . . Although, most likely, the water will be frozen."

The water was frozen, but our driver and two or three of the other men brought the barrel inside, hoping that by morning the water might thaw out.

"Dinner will be served shortly. Take your places." And indeed, in a few moments, several peasant girls entered, carrying huge wooden trays laden with steaming bowls of soup and mounds of freshly baked bread. I had not seen or tasted such delicious food in many months. After we gorged ourselves on several helpings, the commissar advised us to go to sleep.

Tomorrow, early, we were to be on our way to the ice stations. We had very hard times waiting for us.

Dr. Karpova and I spread our sheepskin coats on the floor and cuddled under our army blankets. It was much colder on the floor, but we had no time to think about it. We promptly fell asleep.

In the morning we had more soup and bread. We even had

a chunk of chocolate to eat with our tea. *How Shurik would love a piece of chocolate,* I thought as I ate half of it, saving the other for later. One never knew when we would be given food again, so it was wise to save a bit of energy-giving chocolate for an emergency.

The water in the barrel did thaw out, and we were able to wash our faces and brush our teeth. Our men even shaved, heating the water inside the stoves.

Outside the sun shone brightly. I had to squint in order to face the blinding whiteness of the frozen lake. The sky was brilliantly blue and cloudless. A thermometer at the door read 20° below zero.

"Not too bad," said our driver. "In January it will fall below 40°."

We were issued white robes with hoods to wear over our sheepskin coats for camouflage. Each nurse wore a red cross armband on her left arm.

Behind the barracks was a long caravan of peasant sledges, filled with straw. Thin, exhausted horses were hitched to them, driven by equally thin, exhausted old men—peasants from the neighboring villages.

"Two people to each sledge" commanded our commissar briskly. "Try to remain with comrades from your own hospital."

We settled in the sledges, digging into the straw for warmth. The drivers cracked their whips, and the horses, straining at their harnesses, moved slowly ahead. We were off. The descent onto the ice was very gentle. I didn't even realize that we were traveling on ice until I saw a round crater full of blue water. Our caravan moved along a well traveled route of tightly packed snow. From the opposite direction rolled the long convoys of heavily laden trucks, hastily painted white for camouflage.

The sun was very bright, and the snow sparkled with myriads

of tiny crystals, each glowing like a diamond or a ruby, or an emerald, hurting one's eyes with its brilliance. The air was very clean and brutally cold. I tied a handkerchief across my nose and mouth. I couldn't breathe the air directly. With every gulp I felt a sharp pain in my throat and chest. Riding in a slow-moving open sledge, I felt like a sitting duck. There was no protection from air attack or long-range artillery. There were no shelters, no thick walls. Instead, there were hundreds of feet of icy water below, ready to swallow one up in a moment. Even if one were saved from drowning, one had almost no chance of surviving. The life expectancy of anyone falling into the freezing water was less than ten minutes!

"Are you scared?" I heard Dr. Karpova whisper through her handkerchief face mask.

"Yes. Are you?"

"Yes. Very scared."

We fell silent. It was impossible to talk in this cold anyway. Then we heard planes.

"Here they come, the devils," swore our driver. "Get out of the sledge and lie down on the ice. Quick!" He threw an old white sheet over his horse's back and ran a few steps away from the sledge, throwing himself on the ice. We followed his example without asking questions. The planes came in three waves. They aimed at the truck convoys as they began to drop their bombs.

I lay on the ice, like the driver, face down, terrified into numbness by the deafening explosions and the sounds of rushing water. There were additional explosions as the bombs hit a fuel convoy and tanks of gasoline and oil began to burn. In spite of my fear, I was curious. I lifted my head and looked in the direction of the truck convoy.

Several drivers were lying in the snow, shooting their automatic submachine guns straight at the low-flying planes. I was sure that the drivers felt no fear. They were fighting back instead of meekly awaiting the outcome of the attack. I wished I were one of them. The planes came back for the second time. They strafed the column with machine guns, setting several more trucks on fire.

I heard the wild neigh of a horse as it was hit by a bullet. I saw the poor animal jerk violently and then half fall on the snow, its front quarters hanging limp, still supported by a harness.

Then the Germans were gone. Cautiously the people began to pick themselves up. The damage to the truck convoy was substantial. There were eight or nine trucks burning. The drivers and the soldiers were already swarming around them, trying to salvage whatever was not yet destroyed. There were several craters in the ice, through which I could see the dark-blue water of the lake.

Our own little caravan was miraculously spared. The only casualty was one of the horses. The peasants were busy repacking the load of the fallen horse. The others were working on the carcass itself. They split the belly of the animal and emptied its still-warm internal organs on the snow. Quickly they separated the lungs, the heart and the liver from the pile of bloody, steamy entrails. I had to turn my eyes away, for the picture of these men, digging in the bloody mess with their bare hands, was repulsive. I heard a splash in the water. The peasants dumped the inedible entrails into a shell crater. The carcass was tied behind one of the sledges. The horse meat would not be wasted. There was a huge puddle of red blood on the virginal white of the ice. The peasants hurriedly covered it with heaps of snow, to camouflage the road.

That won't help, I thought. *The Germans can clearly see our road from the air for miles. Maybe even from shore to shore. One look at these disabled or burned trucks and they know where the road is.*

It was true. The enemy knew exactly where the road was. Even the best of camouflage couldn't deceive them. Our trucks moved in a never-ending stream, day and night. Even if by some chance the enemy could not actually see the trucks from the air, they certainly could see the long, grotesque shadows which each truck cast. The sun was never high at this time of year. Shadows were huge, spreading for hundreds of feet, running alongside the convoys like some clumsy, ghostly apparitions from a world of fantasy.

Our caravan trudged along. I saw a group of medics with stretchers, carrying around the stricken convoy, loading the wounded on sledges which were strung together, like shoe boxes in a child's homemade train. Each "train" of six or seven sledges was pulled by a tired, emaciated horse. Obviously the mechanized vehicles were needed for transporting supplies. The wounded had to be moved by a more primitive method.

In spite of fear and cold, I couldn't help but feel curious about my new surroundings. I noticed that about every hundred feet there were small colorful flags stuck in the snow. They were markers to help the drivers follow the road. The ice was still very young and there were many places where little red flags alerted the drivers to a detour.

In some places I saw boards thrown across a shell crater and little flags, fluttering in the wind, warning the drivers of open water. By night the craters would be covered by a newly formed thin crust of ice. In another day or two the boards would be removed and trucks could safely pass once more.

Every few hundred yards I saw traffic controllers, directing the convoys in much the same way as traffic policemen direct traffic on city streets. They were warmly dressed in sheepskin coats and white camouflage robes which reached clear to the snow, covering their dark *valenki*. They wore their snub-nosed

automatic guns slung around their necks and carried extra car-
tridge belts crisscrossing their chests, in the guerrilla tradition.

As we slowly progressed, I noticed machine gun emplacements
and light antiaircraft batteries surrounded by walls of ice blocks.
Everything looked white. Even the guns were painted white in
an attempt to camouflage them. Over each gun emplacement there
hung a net, sagging with a heavy deposit of snow. The gun
crews lived beneath the nets, alongside their batteries.

A platoon of ski troopers ran alongside our caravan. They
wore the familiar white robes. Three of them pulled light sledges
carrying machine guns.

"See those fellows?" the driver turned to us, pointing with the
handle of his whip at the ski platoon. "A few weeks ago they had
dogs to pull those machine guns. But dogs are too smart. They
didn't like to be bombed. They ran away the first time they saw
the Germans drop bombs." The old man cackled, showing his
toothless gums. "You should've seen them. They ran like mad,
pulling the sleds and machine guns with them. So our boys shot
them all and ate them."

"Ate them?" I asked with a shudder.

"Sure. What else were they good for?" the peasant replied with
indifference.

"Weren't they some kind of specially trained, expensive dogs?"

"Dogs are dogs. If they're no good, they're only extra mouths
to feed. In times like these one must think like that," said the
old man with grim conviction. "So, you see, the dumb animals
couldn't stand the bombings. But the smart human beings endure
anything. Now the soldiers, themselves, become the pack animals. See how they pull their machine guns? Far better than
dogs."

We watched as the ski platoon overtook our caravan and soon
disappeared in the whiteness of our surroundings. *Maybe there*

is something in this constant camouflaging? I thought, searching the horizon in vain for the vanished platoon.

The constant hum of the truck engines pulling their loads toward Leningrad suddenly changed. A new sound appeared. We saw huge snowplows, five abreast, move slowly toward us from the opposite shore of the lake.

"Good!" said our driver with satisfaction. "They'll make more roads for our trucks. One or two will never do. The Germans will bomb us right into the lake. No, my girls, to succeed, we must have ten, twenty, forty roads crossing the lake, all full of trucks all the time. Then, if they bomb one or two roads, the rest of them will still be open. If I were the commander of the front, that's what I would do—make a thousand roads over the ice! A whole thousand roads."

In spite of ourselves we laughed. Somehow, the spirit of our driver was contagious, and we felt less depressed. The bustling activity of the Road of Life was in such contrast to the deadliness of the city we left behind that I began to look forward to my two weeks of duty.

By midafternoon we were still traveling.

The commissar, Olga Teleghina, visited with every group of our small convoy, riding for a few moments on each sledge, answering questions, dispelling fears and supplying information. She told us that in an hour, at most, we would arrive at our destination at Kilometer 12 maintenance post.

"Do you ski?" she asked me.

"Yes."

"Good. There are several pairs of skis, and you'll have to make use of them."

"Where are you going to be, Comrade Commissar? At Tikhvin?" asked Dr. Karpova.

"No. Not quite yet. I shall be going back and forth along the

Ladoga road visiting all of you, at least once a day. Later on, when we have our medical line established, I will ask for a transfer to Tikhvin."

She jumped off the sledge, waved us on and waited for the following group to approach her. She stood there in the deep snow, her face almost purple with cold, but her eyes burning with determination under the visor of her cap. She looked like a snowman or, as we say in Russia—*Snegovaya Baba*—for her white robe reached almost to her ankles. Icicles hung from her coat collar where her breath warmed the curly sheep fur.

We moved on and on. Our little horse, its sides bristling with hoarfrost, plodded along, rhythmically nodding its head. The driver dozed, but the horse followed the well trodden furrows from the sledges ahead. I closed my eyes and fell asleep. When I awoke, the sledge stood still. We had arrived at our destination, Kilometer 12.

In front of me I saw three large circular huts built of ice blocks and a courtyard behind a similar wall, where several road maintenance trucks stood under a white canopy.

One of these huts was to be our living quarters for the next two weeks. Dr. Karpova and I jumped off the sledge. Four more girls from our hospital who were to be with us at Kilometer 12 joined us presently. We stood there, staring at the ice huts, feeling lost, not knowing what to do next.

We waited, watching the sledges with medical personnel from other hospitals pass before us. No one seemed to notice us. They all were dozing. At last we saw Olga Teleghina. She leaped from the sledge and came toward us.

"You're the first to settle," said she, through her woolen scarf, which covered her face up to her eyes. "The next post will be five kilometers from here. So the territory you patrol is, roughly, five kilometers in diameter. Good luck, you know your duty."

She raised her arm in a salute and ran off, trying to catch up with the caravan.

"Wait, wait!" Dr. Karpova shouted. "We don't know whom to report to. Who is in command?"

"You are!" she shouted back, jumping on the last sledge. "I'll be back tomorrow!"

She was gone.

"Well, we might as well get inside to see what's what," said Dr. Karpova, resignedly shrugging her shoulders.

We went to the nearest hut. Its entrance was a short, narrow tunnel, only waist high. It was rather difficult to crawl inside dressed in bulky clothing and carrying submachine guns.

Inside, the hut was spacious. It had three wooden platforms with blankets for sleeping and a large table, piled high with boxes of medicaments, bandages and tins of kerosene. There were two large kerosene stoves, which also provided light for the hut, and there was a supply of matches.

"All right, comrades, let's light the stoves first and then see what we've got here," said Dr. Karpova, assuming her command in earnest.

"Won't the hut melt?" timidly asked Parasha, one of our youngest nurses.

"No, silly, it will melt only a little inside, but the frost on the outside will make it even stronger. You've read about the Eskimos, how they keep their fire burning day and night. Well, this hut is built on the same principle; a little melted snow freezes again, acting as cement between the blocks of ice, sealing all crevices," said Dr. Karpova patronizingly. "However, we must hang something at the door . . . This wind is freezing!" Indeed, the cold Arctic wind blew through the doorway, making our stoves flicker and almost go out.

We took one of the blankets and, folding it twice, stuck one end into the crevice over the door. It was still too cold to take off our coats, so we sat around the table, feeling awkward, immobilized by our stiff clothing.

"We'll work in teams of two. Of course, as a doctor, I'll be working with all the teams. But, basically, one team will rest, while the other two are on duty. And now, let's investigate the other huts." All six of us trooped out.

The entrance of the nearest hut, unlike ours, was unprotected by a corridor. There was a deep pile of snow inside. We presumed that it was empty, for the drift at the doorway looked undisturbed.

To our surprise, the hut was full of sleeping men. They must have been utterly exhausted to be able to sleep in such bitter cold, strewn like corpses over every available inch of the floor. Their sleep must have been very deep, indeed, for none of them stirred or responded to our calls.

"Let them sleep, poor souls," whispered Dr. Karpova. "They must be a maintenance crew."

We went to the last hut. No one was inside. But the table within was loaded with boxes of machine-gun ammunition.

"Well, we surely came to the right hut at the beginning," I said. "I would hate to have to move all this heavy stuff from one place to another." We went back to our own hut.

"I wonder when we're going to eat?" said Parasha, expressing the central thought we all had, but hated to be the first to voice.

It was indeed a question of utmost importance. We had had nothing to eat since early morning. It was now nearly four o'clock. We had no rations with us. I still had my little piece of chocolate, but I didn't want to take it out of my pocket for fear of having to share it with the others. I had no feeling of guilt about my selfishness. We Leningraders reached the point where sharing food had become a folly which could cost one's own life. Of course, sharing with Shurik was different. Shurik! I wondered how he was. I knew that he was in good hands with Dr. Stern.

We heard a loud automobile horn, tooting insistently in front of our hut. Parasha left to investigate. "Food!" she yelled excitedly, sticking her head into our doorway. "A whole truckload of hot food!"

We quickly followed her outside. There, right in front of our igloo, stood an old rickety truck outfitted with a field kitchen. Smoke billowed from the tin chimney of a huge round tub. It was covered with an enormous lid, reminding me of a crusader's shield. A young, robust, red-cheeked girl stood next to the tub, with a ladle a yard long in her hands. The dipper end was as big as a large mixing bowl. Another girl, on the ground, presided over a large crate of fresh black bread, still steaming.

"Oh, God, how marvelous!" I cried with exultation. "Soup and bread!"

"Come and get it!" called the girls from the field kitchen. "Where are your containers?"

We had none.

"No matter, we have extras," said the girl on the truck. "You must be new here."

"Yes, we've just arrived from Leningrad," said Dr. Karpova. "We're a medical emergency unit. I'm Captain Karpova, commanding officer."

"Glad to meet you!" smiled the red-cheeked girl. "I'm Sergeant Kukushkina of the supply detachment. Do you have spoons?"

"Yes, we have," said Dr. Karpova. "We were advised to carry our spoons with us always—in our *valenki*."

"That's right!" laughed the supply girls. "It's the best place for a spoon, in the real Russian tradition."

We took our spoons wrapped in pieces of hospital gauze out of our leggings. Traditionally the Russian soldier from all the wars of the past carried his spoon in his leggings. Thus, it was impossible to lose or misplace it.

Sergeant Kukushkina ladled the soup into our new utensils. Each serving was exactly a bowlful. The other girl dispensed the bread.

"Where are the fellows?" asked Kukushkina.

"Sleeping."

"We must wake them up. There will be no more hot food until morning." She sent her helper, who was also the driver of the truck, to sound the horn again. Parasha volunteered to go to the men's hut to wake them.

"You'll have extra bread and sugar for your tea," said Kukushkina to Dr. Karpova. "Tomorrow morning I'll bring hot cereal with butter and more bread."

"With butter!" I exclaimed in happy wonderment.

"Yes, we eat very well here in our ice settlements. You'll even get real meat once in a while. And chocolate. And plenty, plenty of bread."

We all looked at one another with foolish smiles spreading over our faces. Meat! Chocolate! Butter! And plenty of bread! It was unbelievable.

"You'll get two hot meals a day. The rest of the time you must manage with tea and bread. You'll be fat as pigs at the end of your stint here!" joked Kukushkina. Two hot meals! I couldn't believe my good fortune!

Parasha came out, followed by a band of sleepy, unshaven men who immediately surrounded the truck, their outstretched hands holding their soup bowls.

Only now did the soldiers notice us.

"Look! Girls," smiled one of them, pointing at us.

Dr. Karpova frowned. She didn't like to be regarded as a mere "girl." She was a doctor and a captain. She wasn't going to let anyone forget it.

"I'm Captain Karpova," she said severely. "And this is my medical staff. Who is in command of your group?"

"I am," said a middle-aged man, his face all but hidden by his rough whiskers. "I'm Senior Sergeant Maximoff, of the 45th Sapper Corps."

Dr. Karpova's face visibly relaxed. She was superior in rank to everyone. She introduced me. "This is Lieutenant Petrovskaya, my deputy." I shook hands with Sergeant Maximoff. Somehow, here, in our ice settlement, I felt we needed a more informal relationship with our fellow soldiers, instead of the usual stiff saluting and meticulous standing at attention. But our captain thought differently. She wanted no lessening of military discipline.

"Dismissed!" she said coldly. "Take your men back to your quarters, sergeant, before their soup freezes."

The sergeant saluted this young, impudent girl and returned with his men to their igloo. I detected a slightly amused expression on his face as if he were tolerantly indulging the whims of his own little daughter. Our captain, at twenty-three, surely could have been his daughter.

"Take your extra bread rations," yelled cheerful Kukushkina. "I won't be here till tomorrow."

It was a pleasure to watch her work on the top of that truck. She looked like a character from *Grimm's Fairy Tales*, like a marshmallow doll, all round in her padded jacket and pants, covered by a camouflage robe. She looked healthy and gay, as if on a ski holiday rather than in the midst of a deadly winter of war and starvation. Watching her, I began to feel safer, thinking less of the fathomless water beneath the ice, the endless sky from which at any moment enemy planes might appear, sending all of us into the deep, deep lake.

"So long, till tomorrow," Kukushkina said, covering the soup with the crusader's shield with a loud bang. The truck quivered, coughed and finally took off to the next snow settlement. Kukush-kina waved to us with her huge ladle from the top of the truck.

"Quite a girl," I said as I followed Captain Karpova back into our igloo.

"Yes," she agreed. "A very cheerful soul."

"What do we do next? I mean, after we eat our soup?" I asked.

"Three of us will unpack these supplies. The others will put the skis on and reconnoiter the road to get acquainted with our territory."

It seemed strange that we had no specific directives from Medical Headquarters as to our duties and procedures. But then, we had no communication with headquarters at all after Commissar Teleghina deposited us at Kilometer 12. The best we could do under the circumstances was, indeed, to unpack and to investigate our territory.

The Road of Life and an ice hut. Most of the nurses lived in similar huts. *World War II Collection of Seized Enemy Records, National Archives*

6

"We must leave the door open," I said to Dr. Karpova. "We will suffocate in our sleep—all six of us—in this small space, with these two stoves going. What if the stoves go out? We'll be breathing poisonous gas!"

The other girls were already soundly asleep on their pallets. Two of us still sorted the supplies.

"I'd hate to let all this warmth out. In no time it will be as cold as it was when we first came here," she said.

"I know, but just look, we have no ventilation at all. It is already very stuffy, but imagine how it will be by morning."

"I suppose you're right," she agreed slowly. "That's why the men had left their doorway unprotected. All right," she said emphatically, "let's remove the blanket before we go to bed."

But it was easier said than done. The blanket had frozen into the crevice above the door, and all our tugging and pulling came to naught.

"OK, let's leave it where it is. Let's pull the blanket away from the door and put a crate under it. We'll have enough fresh air from each side of the opening, without letting the wind in," suggested Dr. Karpova. I chuckled. "What are you laughing at?" she demanded.

76

"Nothing, really . . . I was just thinking how we all adopted Dr. Stern's idiosyncrasies."

"What do you mean?"

"You, using his 'OK' expression. Thank heaven, the Americans are our allies!"

"Wouldn't it be awful if he were saying *jawohl* all the time." We laughed.

We moved a large crate into the doorway and tucked the end of the blanket under it. It left two triangular openings on each side, through which cold air rushed in. I turned down the wicks on our stoves and curled up on the wooden platform. We all kept our clothes on, except for our *valenki*.

"Good night, Kyra," said Dr. Karpova, using my Christian name for the first time.

"Good night, Zina," I replied, happy that at last our formal relationship was over.

I could hear the deafening blasts of shore batteries. From time to time our little igloo trembled as a shell exploded in our proximity. My roommates continued to rest undisturbed while I, envious of their peace of mind, tossed and turned, trying to capture the evasive sleep.

It must have been close to dawn when I finally fell asleep only to be awakened by Dr. Karpova, who energetically shook me by the shoulder.

"Get up! Time to work! The field kitchen is already here!"

Our first workday on the Road of Life was about to begin.

I attached the ski bindings to my *valenki*. Dr. Karpova handed me my submachine gun.

"Good luck, Kyra," she said solemnly. "We'll be waiting here impatiently for your return."

Parasha and I were the first to go on patrol. The other girls were already busy treating victims of frostbite among the night crews, preparing them for evacuation. During the night the temperature had fallen to 45° below zero. Trucks were unheated, and drivers, forced to sit almost motionless for hours, were badly frozen. Some of them would even have to face amputation of their fingers or toes.

We skied along the road which was choked with trucks. They were moving west in one continuous column toward Leningrad. We headed in the opposite direction. Although we were used to the smooth "Finnish" style of cross-country skiing since childhood, we found ourselves moving jerkily, fighting the skis, clutching to the poles more for support than as a means of propelling ourselves forward. It was hard to ski with a full pack on one's back, with an automatic rifle slung across one's shoulder.

Baptism by fire came soon after our departure from Kilometer 12. We heard the droning sound of airplanes.

"Get away from the road!" I shouted to Parasha. We turned and skied a few yards before we plopped on the snow. We lay there, panting. Methodically the bombs began to fall, nearer and nearer to us. I looked at the sky. There they were. Little dark objects, which grew bigger with astonishing swiftness as they came closer. The bombs screeched before they hit the ice, sending columns of water toward the bright-blue sky.

"I am scared! Mamma!" screamed Parasha, trying to get up.

"Down!" I yelled. "Stay down, you fool!" She dropped on the snow, crying hysterically. I crawled toward her and put an arm around her heaving shoulders. Explosions were all around. The ice below trembled. Though I too felt like Parasha and wanted to run, to hide, I stayed, holding firmly to my hysterical comrade.

I didn't know how long the attack lasted. It might have been a brief few minutes, but the damage was substantial. The ice was pockmarked with dozens of craters, and many trucks were burning. The drivers and the maintenance crews were already swarming around them like an army of white ants, trying to get them rolling again.

"We must be moving, too," I said. "Get up," I said to Parasha sternly. "There are wounded who need us." Like a small, obedient child, her face smudged with tears, she stood up and put her skis on.

We returned to the road, circling around wide cracks in the ice which spread like huge spider legs from the bomb craters. On the side of the road there lay four wounded drivers. We knelt beside them, to give them first aid. There was no time for talking or asking questions. We knew what had to be done.

A horse-driven sledge arrived to pick up our wounded, while we moved on in search of other victims of the attack. Before we were through attending to the last wounded man, there was a second attack. Again we threw ourselves on the snow, only this time Parasha did not scream. Three more such attacks occurred before our patrol duty was over for the day. The Germans were detemined to destroy our road. We were just as determined to keep it open. While the enemy bombed us, a new road a few kilometers north was being built.

The old peasant was right, I thought. *We need a thousand roads to keep the convoys rolling!*

By the end of our shift, we had given first aid to forty-five wounded. We were dog-tired, but Parasha was calm. She had stopped crying, although her body continued to tremble violently with each attack. At home an unpleasant surprise awaited us: our igloo was full of wounded. We had anticipated a bit of rest, a bowl of hot soup and the warmth of our quarters; instead, every available inch was occupied.

"What happened?" I asked Zina. She looked harassed.

"Damned if I know! Apparently, the sledges didn't arrive on time so they all piled up here. I couldn't just throw them out. So I let them wait here."

I looked longingly at my pallet, now occupied by three soldiers.

"Any serious cases?" I asked.

"No. The worst have been evacuated. Anyhow, how was it?"

"Awful. We'll need a small sled to transport our medical supplies. It's too difficult to carry them on our backs."

I found a clear space at the table and settled for a cup of hot tea. For the next four hours I would rest.

The long hours of patrol duty and the short hours of rest stretched into days. We all reached the point where we lost count of time. We could not even tell what date it was. Very often I was confused even about the time of day. If there was no sun, I could not tell whether it was day or night, for the long sub-arctic winter was like one continuous twilight. As for work, there was no difference. We continued to patrol our perimeter around the clock.

Two more roads were opened and our workload increased accordingly. I tried to keep count of the number of wounded we were able to serve. For all three teams in any twenty-four-hour period, we had between 150 to 200 patients. But that was just counting the wounded within our own five-kilometer radius! There were nine or ten other medical units like ours operating along the route. The over-all casualty figures were staggering.

Our commissar, Olga Teleghina, made regular stops at our igloo. She visited us each day, bringing us mail, newspapers, boosting our morale by relating the good news from the front. Bad news she kept to herself. One day she brought me a letter from Shurik.

"Dear Kyra," he wrote, "I miss you a lot. I grew one centimeter. Dr. Stern misses you too. I hope you miss me. Your Shurik Nikanorov." At the bottom of his letter he drew a bouquet of flowers, beneath which he wrote, "These are for you. In the summer I'll bring you real ones."

I tacked the picture onto our wall for all to enjoy. It looked beautiful—our one and only decoration.

Olga Teleghina stared at the picture for a long time. I knew she was thinking of her own children, who had been evacuated to the safety of Kazakhstan, far away from Leningrad. She looked sad.

We invited her to spend a night with us, for it was stormy. The Germans, most likely, would not venture out on such a night. But their long-range artillery continued to shower us with shells. The blizzard outside raged and howled while, for once, we felt safe and cozy inside our icehouse. We were all in—there was no regular patrol duty during the blizzard, although Parasha and I stood by, ready to go out if needed, for the supply trucks kept rolling toward Leningrad—blizzard or no.

"It sure is cozy here," said the commissar, sipping hot tea from her metal cup. "You know what makes it cozy? Shurik's picture. It brings a touch of home, a touch of peace into these grim surroundings."

"I never thought of our igloo as cozy," said Parasha. "I always think of it as some kind of an ice palace. Look how the walls sparkle in this light."

"Ice palace," repeated Teleghina wistfully. "Do you remember the story about the ice palace?" She turned to me.

"Sure, I do. During the time of Empress Anna."

"What ice palace?" demanded Parasha.

"Don't you know? The one which was built on the Neva River to amuse the empress. The one where she held a wedding feast for her two dwarfs?"

"Tell us, please, tell us," begged the girls.

"Please, do tell us." I joined the chorus. "I remember only the basic historic facts about it. There must be more than just that!"

"Oh, all right, I'll tell you," said Teleghina, flattered by our interest. She poured another cup of steaming tea and, looking at the dancing light of a stove, began telling the story.

"You must remember from your history books the time which is known as *Bironovschina*. It was a time of turmoil after the death of Peter the Great, when for brief periods Russia had a series of rulers. Eventually, the nobles of the country decided to invite Peter's niece, Anna, who was the widow of a German princeling, to become the Russian empress.

"Anna, although Russian-born, had lived most of her life in Germany. She didn't trust the Russian nobles advising her on affairs of state.

"She brought a staff of her own advisers from Germany, the most prominent among whom was Biron. The new empress had little interest in affairs of state. She left it to Biron who, to solidify his power, established his own secret police who would report directly to him about malcontents, whoever they might be, high or low.

"Biron was ruthless. The dungeons of the Peter and Paul Fortress were full of prisoners who were tortured and executed in secret without trial. Empress Anna knew nothing of this, or preferred to know nothing.

"She took charge in 1730 and reigned for ten years, during which time she spent enormous sums on banquets and masquerades but nothing on education or public welfare. Arts and sciences, which flourished under Peter the Great, were in danger of extinction.

"But Anna couldn't care less. She danced and entertained,

showering her favorite, Biron, with money, titles, lands and serfs.

"Biron left no stone unturned in order to amuse his bene-factress—at her own expense, of course. Or, rather, at the expense of Russia's treasury, depleted by constant wars.

"So one cold winter, when Empress Anna was particularly bored with the gossip of her ladies in waiting, Biron thought of a new way to entertain her. He decided to have a winter carnival.

"He assembled hundreds of serfs who labored for weeks on the frozen Neva, building a palace of ice blocks. The artisans were ordered to carve furniture and candlesticks, trees and animals, fruits and flowers, all of ice.

"Biron planned to hold an Imperial Ball in the ice palace. But upon hearing that two of the empress's favorite dwarfs were contemplating marriage, he decided to hold their wedding there.

"A gay wedding procession stretched for a mile. The bride and groom, dressed in lavish court costumes of the 18th century, headed the procession.

"Sled after sled, drawn by majestic horses, carrying nobles in masquerade costumes, followed. There were wild horsemen from Kazakhia on little hairy horses, galloping alongside the sleds yelling shrilly, scaring the ladies.

"There were cossacks from the Don and the Dnieper regions in their colorful costumes. There were representatives from every corner of our great country. On special sleds, drawn by fast troikas, rode the ambassadors of foreign countries. They were awed by the lavishness of the procession.

"Then, there were exotic animals which no one had ever seen before. There were elephants, walking slowly, carrying tents on their backs from which strange, dark-featured men, in rich, oriental dress, looked impassively at the gay crowds. 'Look at the Arabs,' shouted the Russians from one to another, pointing to the dark-skinned Hindus, sent to the empress by an Indian potentate. By Russians of the 18th century, every dark-skinned person was considered an Arab.

"There were camels from our own domains in Asian deserts, and lions and tigers in cages. The route of the cortege was lined with thousands of peasants and free citizens of St. Petersburg, dressed in their warmest clothing."

"How I would like to have been there!" exclaimed Parasha dreamily. We all laughed.

"Please, continue!" we begged our commissar.

"Well, Biron was very pleased with the success of his carnival. A ballet was performed in the great ice hall of the palace. The empress was seated on a heap of fur rugs and silken cushions, while the newlywed dwarfs occupied an elaborately carved ice throne. Everyone thought it was a very piquant idea to put the dwarfs on the throne. They were to rule as king and queen of the carnival! The empress was delighted to play the part of a mere 'subject' to their 'Ice Majesties.'

"Servants brought huge platters of intricately arranged fruits and sweets, whole suckling pigs, geese and swans. As the guests tried to carve the food, they discovered that everything was made of ice. The serf-artists created such perfect replicas of delicacies that everyone was deceived, including the empress, who was tempted to try a peach. But the guests didn't mind. They knew that the real feast awaited them in the Winter Palace, minutes away. They laughed heartily, praising Biron for his inventiveness.

"Then the empress expressed her wish to continue the festivities in her own palace. Biron, before following his sovereign, commanded that the ice palace be guarded throughout the night, for he wished to continue the revelries the next day. The dwarfs were left alone, without heat or light, dressed only in their silken costumes.

"By morning they were frozen to death. When the empress

learned this, she said she would miss her dwarfs, who were so good with her pet dogs. But then, they were mere serfs and expendable. They could be bought and sold, exchanged or pawned. It was at a time in our history when we sold human beings. So who cared if two little serfs froze to death?"

"What a terrible story," said Parasha softly. "Poor little people!"

Somehow, before we knew it, our first week in Kilometer 12 was over. I could not say that we got used to the constant bombing and shelling, or spending half our duty hours lying on the snow, waiting for an attack to cease. One couldn't get used to it, but one could learn to bear it and not to think of death.

The enemy tried to recapture Tikhvin, but our troops at the front were reinforced by fresh divisions from the interior of Russia. Tikhvin held. The life-giving rail connection with the rest of our country was firmly in our hands.

Several more ice roads were opened and I learned months later that as many as sixty such convoy routes functioned at one time. The Germans, exasperated by their inability to recapture Tikhvin, intensified their attacks on the Road of Life. They sent wave after wave of bombers to drop their deadly loads on our trucks, our ice settlements and our bases on both shores of the lake.

Camouflage could no longer protect us. Our days became sheer gamble, with the odds against our survival. The first casualty in our group was Commissar Olga Teleghina. On her return trip from Leningrad with another group of medical workers, her convoy was attacked from the air. Eyewitnesses said that the little group was just swallowed up by the lake. The sledge, the horse, the driver, the young nurses and our commissar just disappeared, victims of a direct hit.

We were stunned. We were used to death by now; we had

been living with it in one form or another for months, but the
death of our commissar shook us nevertheless.

It was easier to move without the heavy packs on our backs,
now that we had sleds to carry medical supplies. After the first
week we became more efficient with skis and developed a few
energy-saving methods of our own. We didn't run any longer,
unless there was an emergency. We didn't take our skis off each
time we had to hit the snow, waiting for the air attack to end.
We learned to dive into the snow with the skis still attached to
our *valenki*. Parasha and I went on patrol again.

The death of Teleghina had a terrifying effect on Parasha. She
barely held together under the constant air attacks, but now,
she was near mental collapse. I meant to ask Zina to keep Parasha
in the igloo; not because it was safer—for there was no safety
on the ice for anyone—but because Parasha could not stand the
sight and the sound of falling bombs.

I glanced at the low, gray sky, laden with snow clouds. Maybe,
if we were lucky, the Germans wouldn't fly today. It looked like
another blizzard was in the making. Just then, we heard the drone
of planes. There was a wild look on Parasha's face.

"Steady, Parasha," I said over my shoulder. "They might be
just reconnaissance planes. Bombers have a deeper drone."

We moved off the road, just in case.

Three planes flew low, and we could plainly see the black
crosses on their wings.

"Down!" I shouted, throwing myself on the snow. I heard
machine-gun fire as the planes zoomed low over our heads
strafing the convoy. I heard the bullets hit the ice with that
particular hiss as they made contact with the ice. The planes
banked, ready for another approach. I looked at Parasha, lying
several feet behind me. Her face was down but her body trembled,
shaken by uncontrollable sobs.

I tried to crawl over to her. As I struggled to kick off my skis, the planes returned. Parasha jumped to her feet. She started to run, losing one ski and dragging her supply sled behind her.

"Down! Down! Parasha, stop! Get down!"

She didn't hear. She stumbled blindly ahead. A rapid salvo of machine-gun bullets hit her. She fell on the snow as if someone pulled the rug from under her feet.

"Parasha!" I cried, blinded with tears.

She didn't move. There was a large red spot, growing in size, on the back of her camouflage robe. The planes made the third approach over the convoy and then they were gone. Quickly I ran to Parasha. She was dead.

The tears froze on my eyelashes. I reloaded Parasha's supplies on my sled, stuck the poles of her skis into the snow as a marker and left to attend the wounded. I could do nothing for Parasha. Her body would be picked up by a special platoon. My duty was to help the living.

"Parasha, poor, scared little girl. Why didn't I mention your first outbreak of fear to Zina? Had I reported it then—you might be alive today," I reminded myself.

My fingers were stiff with cold. It was impossible to work with my gloves on. I kept placing my fingers into my mouth, which I found was the best way to keep them from freezing.

Fortunately there were not many wounded. Disobeying orders, I didn't continue on my patrol. I returned to Parasha and towed her to our igloo. We would bury her ourselves. We would bury her in a crater, where we all would probably end up.

A pall of fear hung over the survivors in our igloo. Every time we went on patrol, we felt it would be our last one. Zina joined me on patrol, taking Parasha's place. There weren't many wounded brought to our hut, and she was more needed on patrols. I began to count the hours before we would be relieved from duty.

A new commissar arrived from the front—an elderly man

with the cruel face of a Tartar warrior. We instantly disliked him. He spoke a broken, half-literate Russian, but I was sure that our dislike of Commissar Abdulov was due to the news he brought, rather than his bad Russian. He announced that we were to stay at our stations for an additional week.

"I don't know whether I can last that long," Zina confessed to me during our patrol. "Not only do I feel physically exhausted, but I'm scared, scared all the time."

"I know what you mean," I said. "I feel the same. I feel like Parasha did. I want to run away, to hide somewhere. I know in my mind that it would be the worst thing to do—yet, I can't help it. I want to run away from the bombs. One of these days I will get up and run, just like Parasha."

We looked at each other with compassion. We felt a certain comfort in knowing that we both shared the same fears.

"We'll be back in Leningrad on New Year's Eve. A cause to celebrate—if we survive," Zina said, trying to sound optimistic.

A shell exploded nearby, sending a fountain of water high in the sky. There were cries from the convoy and we skied toward the trucks. One was hit, and it burned furiously. There were bodies of stricken soldiers lying around a new crater. We began to work.

That night we had a visitor, the sergeant from the road maintenance crew, who lived in the next igloo.

We had no contact with our neighbors, the sappers. We all were too busy with our own duties to pay attention to one another. At rare moments of rest, we all fell into deathlike sleep, caring nothing about anybody. But here he was, at our tunnel entrance, asking whether he might enter.

"Sure, come in, if you don't mind our crowded quarters," I said. "I'm Lieutenant Petrovskaya."

"I remember," he said, shaking hands with me.

"What brought you in?" asked Zina, not unkindly.

"I need your help," he said. "One of the men in our hut is ill. He is feverish and delirious. Can you take a look at him, doctor?"

"But of course," said Zina Karpova. "Is he wounded?"

"No, no, he is just ill. Actually he is not one of my men. He is a naval officer, sent to Ladoga on an inspection. He became ill in our section of the road. We took him in, thinking he might feel better by morning. Instead, he became worse, so I must call on you for help."

"I'm glad you did," said Zina, putting her coat on. "Let's go."

The sergeant and Zina crawled out of the igloo. I straightened up the table and washed the dishes. There was plenty of water in our hut. There was always a fresh supply of snow outside that could be melted into water. I looked with envy at the two sleeping girls. How I wished I could curl up under a blanket and sleep for twenty-four hours.

There were noises at the entrance to our tunnel, and I lifted the blanket to see who was there. In the darkness outside I could barely make out the outlines of several people.

"Who's there?" I called.

"It's I," replied Zina. "We're bringing the patient in. Prepare one of the pallets."

All we need—a sick man in our hut, I thought with irritation. Each time we had to share our hut with the wounded it meant inconvenience and additional hardships for us. We had to give up our pallets for them, had to share our own food and water. Not to mention the inconvenience of performing our natural functions. We had a latrine bucket at the far end of our igloo, the use of which became impossible for the duration of the patients' stay in our quarters.

With all our sympathy for the suffering wounded, we couldn't help but hate to have to share our igloo with them, even for a short time.

Zina backed into the igloo, like a crab. She pulled a blanket on which a man lay covered with his sheepskin coat. The sergeant pushed the man through the tunnel by his shoulders, crawling behind him on all fours. Another man came behind them, bringing the sick man's service pistol and a shoulder dispatch case.

We lifted the officer onto the pallet.

"We'll be going," said the sergeant. "Thanks, I know he is in good hands. I'll telephone headquarters in the morning to request that he be evacuated."

"Telephone?" I asked, with incredulity. "Do you have a telephone?"

"Yes." He beamed. "We finally got our own field telephone. Our code name is *Goloobka,* a little dove."

"Sounds very romantic," said one of our nurses awakened by the commotion.

"When did you get your telephone?" I insisted. "We tried and begged and couldn't get even a promise of one."

"We got it today. You're welcome to use it whenever you need to." We thanked the sergeant, and he left, accompanied by his comrade.

Our attention turned toward our new boarder. He was in a coma. He breathed laboriously. His pale face was wet with perspiration. He was a handsome man, in spite of his sick pallor and growth of tough whiskers. He must have been very tall, for his feet protruded over the edge of our pallet.

"I know him," said Zina quietly, as if afraid that he could hear. "He is Vladimir Kuznetzov, my brother's friend from the Naval Academy."

7

There were only four of us left. In addition to Parasha, Tamara had been killed in action, too. Thus, we doubled our efforts. Lieutenant Kuznetzov was evacuated a week later. He was still delirious and unable to recognize Zina. We bundled him up, hoping that his strong constitution would carry him through. With all compassion for the sick officer, I couldn't help but feel relieved that our hut was once again for us only.

The days just before we were to be replaced were the longest. We began to save our bread and chocolate so that we could bring a little hoard of provisions back to Leningrad where we would have to return to starvation rations.

Our friend from the field kitchen, Sergeant Kukushkina, brought us a whole ham as a parting gift.

"Where did you get it?" we queried. She only laughed, showing her neat, white teeth.

"Never mind! Just eat it and enjoy it."

"She stole it," said her helper. "We came upon a bombed food supply truck. The soldiers were reloading it, so there was plenty of stuff laying around."

"So I grabbed the ham and ran," laughed Kukushkina. "The guys yelled at us, but we just stepped on the gas."

"Don't you want it for yourselves?" asked Zina.

"We have another one!" laughed the helper. "Kukushkina grabbed two hams."

"Might as well. The punishment for stealing would be the same for one as for two," she explained cheerfully.

"What's the punishment?" Zina was curious.

"A firing squad," said Kukushkina simply.

"A firing squad!" We couldn't believe our ears.

"Sure! Imagine if everyone stole something? There would be nothing left at the end of the day! So they must be tough with thieves. They must shoot them to make an example for the others." She sounded very self-righteous, and obviously she approved of the punishment.

"But what about you? Aren't you afraid that they might have caught you, too?" I wanted to know.

"Oh, no, we don't do it often. Besides, we didn't steal. We didn't hide in the dark and steal something secretly. We just took the hams. We took them openly, for everyone to see. If the soldiers wanted to stop us, they could have done so easily. We just took them and drove away. Of course, if an officer were there— then, he might have had us arrested."

"But we looked to see whether there was an officer," the other girl broke in. "There wasn't."

"Anyhow, eat your ham and enjoy yourselves." Kukushkina climbed aboard. The truck was gone in a cloud of exhaust.

"Well, let's do as Kukushkina advised," said Zina, carrying the ham into the igloo.

December thirtieth was our last day at Kilometer 12.

It started as a gray, bitter morning, with ferocious winds blowing swarms of powdery snow into great snowdrifts. The trucks on the road continued to roll with the never-ending groan of their tired engines. But now, the trucks returning from Leningrad were also filled to capacity.

They carried refugees from the city. When some days ago we saw a group of refugees for the first time, we were appalled. We forgot how deathly their faces looked, how huge were their eyes, sunken inside their dark, deep sockets. They were a motley crowd, dressed in several layers of clothing, draped in their blankets in Indian fashion. They were allowed to carry only a few kilograms of luggage. There were strict regulations about the size and form of bundles. They wore what they could on their backs, both for warmth and to permit them to hand-carry more.

"How are the things back in Leningrad?" I asked a woman refugee. Her truck was stopped on the road in a traffic jam in front of our hut.

"Bad. Although the government increased our rations on Christmas day, the people keep dying. It's too late for them. I mean, the increase."

"How much did they increase the rations?"

"By 100 grams of bread for workers and 75 grams for all others, including children."

"Well, it's better than nothing," I said. "At least it is an extra slice of bread. It will boost morale, more than anything."

"For many it's too late. They keep dying," insisted the refugee, with a dull expression on her face. The poor soul must have been near death herself. I could see the horrible marks of dystrophy on her skull-like face, her clawlike hands. The dullness of her speech and the slowness of her reactions were telltale signs of an often fatal condition.

The truck engine roared. The refugees grabbed one another for support. Once again they moved on, away from Leningrad, away from death and starvation, on, to the safety of the mainland. But I knew that for some of them this short journey over the lake would be their last. Many of them would die for they were beyond saving.

As I watched the never-ending stream of vehicles from both directions on our last day at the post, a truck pulled up in front of our compound. Commissar Abdulov alighted.

"I brought your replacements," he announced. "Introduce the new girls to their duties. I'll be back shortly with the sledges to take you to Osinovetz."

A group of six nurses awkwardly climbed down from the rear of the open truck. Their faces were purple with cold, and their eyelashes and brows were covered with frost.

"Get inside, comrades, you must be frozen stiff." Zina pointed to the entrance of our igloo.

We were eager to transfer our duties to them as soon as possible. Yet, we saw the fear and anxiety on their faces, and we remembered how we felt the first day.

"You'll get used to it," I said, as a shell exploded near our compound and the little igloo trembled.

"How many people from your group did you lose?" asked one of the new nurses.

Zina and I exchanged glances. We wished we could have said "none," but we had to tell the truth.

"Two," said Zina.

"One third of your group," slowly reflected the new nurse. "It's too many."

We let the remark pass. What good was it to try to explain the situation? How could we really minimize the danger? Why should we?

We packed our few belongings and divided our hoarded food equally. The new nurses watched enviously the disappearance of chocolate and ham into our knapsacks.

"The field kitchen will be here in an hour or two." I watched their hungry faces. "We can't spare any of our food. We have families back in Leningrad."

"You'll have plenty of food while here at Kilometer 12," Zina said reassuringly. "At the end of your stay you, too, will be able to take something home. I'm sorry that we can't share with you." The new nurses protested that they really didn't expect that.

Though practically starving, they still clung to traditional Russian manners, denying that one ever was in need of anything.

"How often do you go on ski patrol?" the commanding officer of the new group, Lieutenant Shilova, asked.

Zina hesitated. She didn't want to bring up our losses again but there was no other way.

"When we had six people in our group we were able to work three eight-hour shifts. Now, with only four left, we go on patrol every other six hours. It's tough," she concluded.

"Until our first casualty we'll follow your schedule," said Lieutenant Shilova dryly. She was a tall, thin girl with dark hair and deep-brown eyes. She looked like a gypsy. Her long, bony wrists protruded from the sleeves of her much too short tunic. Her hair, cropped close to her head, made her appear vaguely masculine. She must have been very exotic-looking before the war. She reminded me of American fashion models—thin, boyish, tall and graceful. Even now, in her ugly ill-fitting army uniform, with face drawn and eyes sunken, she still looked handsome.

"What were you before the war, lieutenant?" I asked impulsively.

"What? Oh, yes, before the war I was a dancer in the Leningrad Folk Dancing Ensemble. Why?"

"I knew it," I exclaimed triumphantly. "I just knew it. You look too elegant to be a regular army nurse."

"How are you going to manage without a physician?" Zina

broke in. I suspected that her vanity was hurt when she learned that she was succeeded by a mere nurse.

"Medical Headquarters knows that with the additonal new roads and trucks it is relatively easy to get to Novaya Ladoga and other points on the eastern shore. They need doctors at the hospitals there, rather than here at first aid stations," said Shilova. She didn't mean to diminish Zina's work at Kilometer 12, but I feared that my friend took it that way.

"You'll be surprised at how many serious cases requiring a doctor's immediate attention you'll have here," she said abrasively. "You'll be sorry that you don't have a physician on the spot."

"Tell me, what about this rumor about food increase in Leningrad?" I asked, changing the subject. "I've heard that people are now receiving three slices of bread daily in addition to a little fat and sugar. Is that true?"

"Oh, yes," said Shilova. "Not only did they increase our rations, but they opened several feeding stations, *stazionari,* as well to help people regain their health. They are nutrition centers. People go there, as if to a restaurant, and they are given a bowl of soup or even a full dinner of soup and mashed potatoes, tea with sugar and bread."

"Is it in addition to their regular rations?"

"Yes. They are given special coupons which they redeem at the *stazionari*. Most of the big factories which still operate in Leningrad have opened *stazionar*i of their own. But there is one in particular, in the Astoria Hotel, which is opened for the intelligentsia only—for writers, composers, actors, artists. They say that some of the intellectuals had to be brought in on stretchers, they were so weak."

"Of course, they were always given the lowest rations. They must have been the first to go down with dystrophy."

"But why?" Shilova demanded. "Why would the intellectuals get the lowest rations? Why, for instance, would our choreographer, Barsov, get less bread than some Ivan Ivanov, who happened to be a factory worker? Our Barsov is the only one! His talent is far more important to our country than some faceless Ivanov of whom we have millions."

"In time of war we have more need for faceless Ivanovs, as you put it, than for all the talents of your dancing teacher," Zina broke in tersely. "We ought to think first of our workers and soldiers. They must fight the war. The rest of the population, particularly the men who are not in the armed forces, must pay in some way for the safety of rear-echelon jobs. Thus the food-ration discrepancies."

She was right, of course, but I couldn't help disliking her haughty attitude and patronizing tone.

Natasha and Vera, our remaining comrades, arrived from their patrol, bringing with them a huge tin of butter.

"Where did you get that?" sharply demanded Zina. "Did you steal it?" She was obviously in a foul mood.

"No, no! Honestly, we didn't!" said Vera. "A driver gave it to us for bandaging his hand."

"What was wrong with his hand?" Suspicious as always, Zina wouldn't let the girls go. "Was he wounded?"

The girls hesitated and then spoke at the same time. "Yes." "No."

"Which is it then, yes or no?" the doctor demanded severely.

They didn't speak. They looked down, their faces flushed from exposure to the frost. Or was it the blush of embarrassment?

"He said he had sprained his wrist," said Natasha haltingly. "So we made a splint for him."

Zina looked at them sharply.

"But you, really, don't think so, do you? I mean, you suspect that his wrist is all right, that he just faked it? Isn't it so?"

The girls nodded miserably.

"So you made a splint for him. And, for your kindness, he gave you a tin of butter. Of stolen butter."

The girls nodded once again, still not daring to meet her awesome stare.

"You took a bribe," whispered Zina dramatically. "You, the members of the Young Communists, you took a bribe! No, you didn't steal! You're much too noble to steal. You just let someone else do your stealing for you! Do you remember what the punishment is for stealing?" she thundered. "It is death by a firing squad, that's what the punishment is!" she hissed, falling back to a stage whisper.

Zina was very effective in her tirade. She reminded me of Don Basilio from the Barber of Seville. He would start his aria about defamation of character in a whisper and go to a thundering crescendo as the aria progressed to its threatening climax. It was always very rewarding to watch this progression of moods.

Vera and Natasha were in tears.

"It is too late to catch the louse, this thieving, lying driver. But you two are still here," Zina concluded menacingly.

There was a commotion at our entrance, and presently Commissar Abdulov's broad Tartar face came into view under the folds of the blanket curtain.

"The sledges are here," he announced. "Let's go; I want you to reach the shore before dark."

"Pack your gear and let's go," said Zina calmly to the culprits, not giving a hint about the drama which just took place.

"What about the butter?" I murmured, pointing with my eyes to the tin. I wished she would say, "Let's take it along."

"Lieutenant Shilova, please accept this butter as our welcome gift. We won't have any need for it," Dr. Karpova said in a formal tone of voice, handing the tin to our replacement commander.

"Do you really want us to have it?" Shilova couldn't believe her ears. A whole tin, five kilograms of butter! It was ten times more than the monthly ration of fats for all eleven of us gathered in the hut.

"Yes, I do," Zina said coldly.

The commissar, too, was surprised, but for a different reason.

"Where did you get this butter?" he asked, with hostile suspicion. As a political observer it was his duty to watch over military discipline and to promptly report any wrongdoing.

"We found it in the snow after a raid," smoothly lied Zina.

"Then why didn't you return it to the supply convoy?"

"Which convoy? We didn't know which convoy it came from."

"Then why are you leaving it behind?" he demanded.

"Just to make life a little bit more pleasant for our replacements," she said with hauteur.

We shook hands with the new occupants of our igloo and crawled out. Two sledges, drawn by horses, each with a peasant driver, were waiting for us.

"We must say good-by to the maintenance crew," I said. We went to their igloo, but it was empty. They were on the road.

"Say good-by for us," Zina said. "They were good neighbors. They let us alone." Lieutenant Shilova promised to give them our regards.

Zina and I climbed into the first sledge, while Natasha and Vera, avoiding looking at us, settled in the other.

"Good-by," we shouted to Abdulov and the new crew. They waved to us as the sledge began to move. We looked back. Two of the new girls were adjusting skis to their *valenki*, ready to go on patrol.

"What are you going to do about them?" I asked, indicating Natasha and Vera.

"Nothing. I can't denounce them. If I do—they might indeed

shoot them. Let them be scared. It will be their punishment."
Then she looked at me sharply. "Don't you dare to say a word
about it to them! I want them to feel scared. Promise?"

"Promise," I smiled behind my handkerchief mask. "I knew
that you couldn't have meant what you were saying about the
firing squad."

Our trip back to Osinovetz took only three hours, due undoubtedly to our sprightly horses. In Osinovetz a half dozen new
buildings had sprung up at the approaches to the woods. There
were new warehouses and landing platforms, all painted in dirty
white camouflage designs. The walls of the warehouses looked
as if painters were let loose to create abstract murals.

We bade good-by to our driver and patted his horse. The mare
looked at us from the corner of her eye and neighed.

"Give her a piece of sugar," said the peasant. "She's a good
horse." He reached into the pocket of his coat and gave us each
a cube of dirty sugar, covered with curly sheep hair. The horse
greedily scooped the sugar from our extended palms with her
warm, wet lips.

Natasha and Vera were waiting for us, timidly huddling
together. Zina ignored them, but I said over my shoulder, "Let's
go. We must find out about transportation to the city."

"Why don't we hitch a ride?" suggested Zina. "Hundreds of
trucks go there constantly. The drivers will be glad to give us a
lift."

It sounded like a good idea. Presently a huge truck slowly
pulled up and stopped in front of us. A friendly face appeared
in the window.

"Want a ride to the city?" shouted the driver.

"Sure! Can you take two?" yelled Zina.

"Get in!" The driver's companion moved over as Zina beckoned Natasha and Vera to climb into the truck. "Report to me

at the hospital tomorrow," she ordered crisply. Then, smiling to the driver, she shouted, "Thank you, comrade, for helping us. Too bad you have no place for two more!"

"Wait for truck number sixty-one! My buddy is driving it. It's like mine—big."

We waited a few minutes. Then I spotted number sixty-one painted on the fender of the approaching truck. We waved our arms until the driver stopped.

"Comrade driver, would you mind giving us a lift to the city?" Zina said.

"With pleasure," said the driver. "Climb aboard." His helper had already cleared a space for us.

We were seated in the cab in no time, holding our guns between our knees and our packs on our laps. It was crowded in the cab, but it was very warm.

We introduced ourselves. When they learned that we were officers, they became restrained and embarrassed. The traditional gap between officers and noncoms was as wide as always. I tried to chat with the soldiers, asking them questions about their work, but they answered in a formal manner. It made a chat impossible.

Soon I gave up my attempts. *Might as well take a nap,* I thought, glancing at Zina, whose head kept nodding, for she was already asleep. I placed my chin on the parcel on my lap and closed my eyes.

8

We arrived in Leningrad at twilight. The convoy stopped at the outskirts of the city. The driver woke us up.

"Here we part company. We're not allowed to carry passengers within the city," he said.

We shook hands with the men, then helped one another adjust our knapsacks. We had to keep our arms free. We were back in the city, where bandits lurked in the darkness of the bombed-out streets. We had a long way ahead of us, ten or twelve kilometers, at least, before we would reach the hospital.

The truck convoy was gone. We were alone. In the silence of the foreboding city our footsteps seemed almost loud, despite the soft soles of our *valenki*. The hard-packed snow crunched under our feet. We had the unpleasant feeling that the noise we made was heard by some unseen foe. It was only five o'clock in the afternoon, but the city looked dark as midnight.

In peacetime, electric lights would be shining. Streetcars, clanking merrily, would be rushing crowds of people home from work. Now there were only the two of us, walking in the middle of the street, keenly attuned to any suspicious noise, ready to use our guns. Our beautiful city, our Leningrad, lay in wait for us, as if it were our enemy.

We walked for an hour without encountering a soul. Then, we heard footsteps. Instinctively we reached for our guns.

"Your papers, please." A tall soldier, accompanied by two girls in militia uniform, flashed a small beam of light into our faces. "Where are you bound, comrades?" he queried.

"To the military hospital on Griboyedov Canal," Zina replied.

"It's a far way from here. It'll take you at least a couple of hours," said the soldier. "It's dangerous near the river. Only yesterday a band of deserters attacked three civilians returning from the Road of Life, carrying bundles of food they had saved while on duty. The filth murdered them, right on the bridge."

"What shall we do then?" asked Zina. "We must cross the river."

"You can remain with us," said the soldier. "In half an hour we cross the bridge ourselves, so we can take you there. Our headquarters is on the other side," he explained.

We looked at each other. It sounded like a good idea.

"All right," said Zina. "We'll go along."

We joined the patrol. As we got closer to the populated area, we encountered more people. Mostly they were soldiers who were on pass to visit their families. Some of them had just been released from hospitals. We stopped them all and checked their military papers.

Only occasionally did we see a civilian, usually a woman, pulling the inevitable child's sled carrying water containers, or a corpse swaddled in a sheet.

"People keep on dying, don't they?" I asked.

"Oh, yes. In our district we had close to 10,000 deaths during this month alone."

"But I understand that there was an increase in food rations,"

Zina said. "Didn't it help?"

"Not much. It will be months before the increase in rations and the opening of feeding *stazionari* will have any radical effect on the populace. You see, when people are weakened to the point of dying from lack of food, a few more grams of bread won't save them. It's too late for them," the patrolman explained.

"Also," one of the militia girls broke in, "don't forget those thousands of unfortunates who lost their ration cards. Either they were robbed, or they lost their cards during the bombings. They would be the first to die from starvation."

"Don't they get duplicate cards?" I asked.

"No. Only those who can really prove that they indeed lost their cards ever get a replacement. The majority must wait until the first day of the next month for their new card."

"But it is cruel," I cried.

"At the militia headquarters we have long lists of bombed buildings. We tried to reissue the ration cards to those who lost them due to bombings. But you would be surprised how many people request new cards, though they are not entitled to them."

"Do they ever get away with it?" I asked.

"They used to. But not anymore. Now we have a new rule. No cards issued to anyone—except at the regular time, on the first of the month."

"Then, despite the increase in supplies over the Road of Life, are people still dying?" asked Zina.

"It will be a long time before the city begins to notice the difference," said the soldier. "There are just too many of us trapped here."

We reached the bridge. It was empty of all traffic. It stretched before us, lonely and majestic, the once elaborately gilded lamp-posts looking dark in camouflage paint. Most shiny surfaces in the city had been repainted: the cupolas of the St. Isaac and

Kazan cathedrals, numerous churches and spires, they all were given coats of protective dark paint.

Across the river we parted company with the friendly patrol. We still had a long way to go, but now we walked along streets more familiar to us.

The moon finally rose and illuminated our way. It shone on the dark apartment houses which looked deserted. Not a spark of life. Not a sound. It was hard to believe that behind the dark façades of the houses lived nearly three million people. Complete silence—only the sound of crunching snow under our feet.

The cloudless sky was filled with antiaircraft balloons. Every evening at dusk, hundreds of huge balloons rose into the sky, hanging above the city like fat whales suspended in the atmosphere. Some of them had trailing antiaircraft nets; others floated at varying altitudes. I doubted whether they ever really stopped the enemy, but just seeing them gave one a suggestion of security.

"A night like tonight is made for air raids," said Zina.

"Sh-sh-sh. Don't talk like that," I whispered quickly. Like all Leningraders, I grew superstitious. We believed that even the thought of an attack could bring the real thing.

It was nearly eight o'clock. We had been in Leningrad for three hours now. I had no hope of seeing Shurik tonight. By the time we reached the hospital he would be asleep. *But I'll see him,* I thought. *I'll see him, even though he doesn't know it.*

My knapsack felt heavy. I tried to shift the weight from the small of my back to the shoulder blades, but lost my balance and fell, sprawling on the slippery, uneven street. My knee hurt. I must have twisted it as I fell. I limped on, angry that our progress toward the hospital was slowed down because of it. The nearer we came to the hospital, the more excited we became. Was it still there?

We passed the silent silhouette of my apartment building.

Thank heavens, it stood intact. I felt Zina's friendly squeeze on my arm. I knew what it meant. She was congratulating me that my house was still there, undamaged.

We passed the bombed building where I found Shurik. One more turn, and we would be in front of our hospital. Would it be there? We had had no letters from the city ever since Commissar Teleghina had been killed. There were rumors that a large hospital in Leningrad was burned to the ground. Could it have been ours?

Instinctively we began to walk faster; I, limping with every step, keeping up with Zina, who generously gave me her shoulder for support. The last turn, and there it was, our hospital, dark, silent, seemingly deserted, but undamaged. We stopped and embraced each other, smiling foolishly. I never knew how much this building meant to me.

"Come on, let's go," cried Zina impatiently. We climbed the few broad steps leading to the front door. Zina opened it, and a wave of stale sour air, smelling of medications and human bodies, struck us, making us reel. We had become accustomed to living in the cold clean air at the lake.

"Whew! What a stink," said Zina with revulsion.

In the flickering light of a tallow candle placed in a saucer on the table in the reception room, I could see her pretty nose quiver in disgust. I smiled. The ugly candle. Our homemade candle. We were home, at last. I eased the knapsack from my shoulders and sat on the bench.

"Is anyone here?" Zina raised her voice authoritatively. "Imagine, the doors are unlocked, and there's no one in the reception room!" Dr. Karpova was back in her own element.

We heard footsteps, and presently two nurses carrying tin cups of steaming tea walked into the room.

"Why is there no one on duty in the reception room?" queried Zina sharply.

The young nurses were new to me.

"And who are you to yell at us?" challenged one of them spunkily.

"I'm Dr. Karpova, the deputy hospital commander," she said icily, "and who are you?" The girls visibly shrunk with fear.

"We are—we are new here. We just went to get some hot water. We were here all the time, honestly," one of the girls said.

"You are to report to me tomorrow," Zina ordered dryly. The nurses, their young faces blanched with fear and anticipation of punishment, silently nodded their heads.

We left them to their thoughts about their future which at the present appeared to them rather bleak. As any member of the *Komsomol*—the young Communists—knew, leaving one's post was tantamount to treason.

We ascended the stairs leading to Dr. Stern's office, and Zina knocked.

"Come in," came the reply in the familiar gruff tone.

Dr. Stern was sitting at his desk. The room was in semidarkness. The only light was provided by three square candles placed in a row on his desk. The old face of our chief looked tired and even older than I remembered.

In the corner of the room I could see a cot on which was a sleeping child.

"My dear girls," exclaimed Dr. Stern with his arms outstretched, like an old grandfather greeting his long-missed grandchildren. We threw ourselves into his arms as if we were, indeed, two little girls visiting their beloved *dédushka*.

He kissed and hugged us, laughing happily.

"Thank God, you are safe!" he kept repeating, fussing around us, helping us with our sheepskin coats, rushing over to his stove to fill our cups with hot tea.

"And Shurik is fine, too," he cried happily, patting me on the shoulder. "He missed you a lot at first, but we kept him busy."

I went to the cot. The child slept soundly, covered with Dr. Stern's overcoat for extra warmth. I was home, among my friends again. I felt safe and happy. Behind the darkened windows an artillery shell exploded, shaking the hospital. Shurik didn't stir.

It was easy to get back into the routine of my work. Nothing had changed at the hospital: the same wounded, hundreds of them, with the same faces, the same wounds, the same cries of pain and anguish.

My reunion with Shurik took place next morning, on my birthday. He burst into the nurses' dormitory, carrying a huge flower which he made from crinkly tissue paper.

"It's for you," he cried, pushing the flower into my hands. "Happy birthday!"

"Wait, wait," I laughed, getting up from my cot. "Let me look at you!" He threw himself into my arms, burying his face in my neck.

"I am so glad you're back," he whispered in my ear. "I worried about you."

I squeezed him tightly. "I was worried, too," I whispered to him.

I kept looking at my little boy, so thin and fragile, his head shorn of hair, his eyes huge in his emaciated face.

The other nurse, awakened by Shurik's arrival, smiled at us. "He was a good boy while you were away," she said. "Everyone here likes Shurik. He is very useful."

I looked at him with pride. I knew that he would be, for he was mature beyond his years.

"Run along and attend to your duties. I'll see you later, and we'll go home together tonight," I said.

"Happy birthday, Kyra," said Zina, entering the dormitory. "I have a present for you, but I'll give it to you tonight, at your party."

"May I come to the party?" the nurse said pleadingly.

I didn't know Lucya too well, but I felt embarrassed by our mentioning the party in her presence. So I said, "Sure, come along."

"But bring your own bread and sugar rations," said Zina coldly, casting an angry glance at me.

"Oh, yes, of course. I wouldn't dream of sponging on you," Lucya cried happily. "I haven't been to a party since before the war!"

"Nobody has," said Zina icily, extinguishing Lucya's enthusiasm instantly.

I dressed quickly, gulped my tea and bread sprinkled with sugar brought to me on a tray by Shurik.

"Eat all of it. It's good for you," he said, like a grown-up.

I smiled to myself. My little boy was adopting the fatherly tones of Dr. Stern. I went into the wards. Yes, everything felt the same, as if I had never been away. The same sour smell, the same absence of electricity and water. The same tired faces of overworked nurses.

I came to the noncom ward.

"How is Polivanov?" I asked the nurse on duty.

"The same. For a while, right after the operation, he was better, but then, he had a relapse."

"Gangrene?"

"Not yet, but Colonel Stern thinks that it is unavoidable."

I went to Polivanov's bed. His face was flushed, and he breathed heavily. His eyes were open, but he didn't seem to be awake.

"He is like this most of the time," whispered the nurse. "We don't even know whether he understands anything."

The other wounded, upon seeing us, besieged us with requests for water, tea, bedpans and pain-killing medicine. Two or three of them asked for Shurik. He, it seemed, had promised to write letters for them. When every request was satisfied or pacified, we left the ward.

I would be more careful not to get caught in ward duties. I was due in surgery in five minutes and I hadn't even scrubbed yet.

It was eight o'clock at night when Shurik and I were finally able to leave the hospital. I limped on, using Shurik's narrow little shoulder for support along the slippery streets.

We arrived at our apartment, noting with relief that all padlocks were intact. No one had broken into our room during our absence. The room was icy. When I lighted the candle, the walls sparkled with tiny crystals of frost.

"Don't take your coat off until its gets warmer," I warned Shurik, lighting the stove. Thank heavens, I still had enough wood left to keep the stove going for the whole evening.

"It's good to be home," said Shurik, unloading our packages on the table.

"Sure is." I smiled.

Through the loudspeaker of the Leningrad radio, hanging on my wall, came the faint sound of a metronome. This methodical ticktock kept reminding us, the people, that there were still communications between us and the rest of the country. Although we had no electrical power to light our homes or to heat our buildings, there was still enough left to connect us by radio with the city authorities. We heard the news—all bad—and we learned of approaching air raids. And it was the radio, too, that announced the welcome all-clear signal. When there was no special program of music or poetry reading, the steady beat of the metronome was broadcast to inform us that we were not alone, or forgotten. The radio was never silent.

Now, as we prepared for my birthday party on New Year's

Eve, the sound of the metronome was particularly pleasant. I knew that soon there would be a broadcast from Moscow. Maybe even a special holiday program of music and songs.

Shurik and I were anticipating our party with relish. We had plenty of food from my lake supplies, and we looked forward to gorging ourselves. All the guests were to bring their own food. Thus we didn't have to share any of our own.

The room was warming up. The frost on the walls began to melt, and tiny drops of water trickled down the wallpaper. There was a knock at the door. Our guests were arriving. Dr. Stern, Zina and Dr. Yakovlev, a new doctor sent to us just before we left for Ladoga, all came together. Somewhat later, Lucya arrived, accompanied by the one-legged Commissar Churakov. I was glad I had thought to invite him. He seemed to be so lonely at the hospital.

"Sit down, sit down, my friends," I fussed, limping around. I felt so happy to have guests in my room.

Shurik put his paper flower into a crystal vase and placed it in the center of the table.

"Do you like it?" he asked me in a fierce stage whisper.

"Beautiful."

"I brought you a present," said Dr. Stern, reaching inside his sheepskin coat. "Here is a bottle of good, prewar port. We'll drink it to your health."

"I have a present also," said Zina. "I know that you like Hemingway. Here is his Farewell To Arms. I inscribed it for you." She handed me a Russian translation of my favorite American author. Inside, she wrote, "To my dearest friend, without whom the days on the lake would have been unbearable." I felt touched to the point of tears. I was never sure that Zina, so aloof, so distant, really liked me.

"I have a bottle of vodka for you to commemorate your birthday," said Commissar Churakov.

"And I a can of sardines," joined Lucya.

"I also have a little contribution to make," said Dr. Yakovlev, who was silent until then. "I have a quarter of a pound of real coffee."

Suddenly I couldn't stand it anymore. I began to cry. I pressed my face against the rough fabric of Dr. Stern's tunic and let the tears roll. These kind people, showering me with such priceless gifts.

"Why are you crying? You should be happy that we have mountains of food. And you are crying," Shurik admonished me soberly.

Zina and Lucya volunteered to make coffee. Luckily I still had a whole bucket of water from the days before I left for the lake. It was solidly frozen, and it had to be thawed out before we could use it.

I wiped my tears and stood up. *No more foolishness. I mustn't allow self-pity,* I thought, embarrassed by my moment of weakness.

The radio metronome stopped. The sonorous voice of the radio announcer said, "*Govorít Moskva,* Moscow speaking." We hushed. As if enchanted, we stared at the dull-black paper cone, as if expecting some miraculous news, some glorious announcement. The end of the blockade? The end of the war? Of course, we knew better than that. Only minutes ago, we were subjected to the enemy's vicious artillery barrage and felt our city tremble. The Nazis wanted to remind us that there would be no Happy New Year for us, if they could help it.

We heard the sound of the Kremlin chimes. Then, the music of the national anthem, as it spread through the airwaves from Moscow. When it was over, Dr. Stern rose to his feet.

"Happy New Year, comrades," he said quietly. "Happy birthday, Kyra. Let's drink a toast to our future . . . to the end of the war . . . the end of all wars." I knew he was overwhelmed with emotion.

"To the future!" yelled Shurik, raising his tiny glass of wine. The heavy, solemn atmosphere was gone. Grateful that the tension was broken, we began to smile, touching glasses of vodka with one another in the old Russian tradition.

Our table, laden with food, had the festive appearance of almost prewar plenitude. We had seven portions of black bread, four slices of Kukushkina's stolen ham, one can of sardines and a small chunk of salted pork. In addition, we had a few chips of chocolate, a can of condensed milk, and a whole quarter of a pound of butter. And coffee!

Truly, it was a feast.

Beyond the walls of my room the cold, dark night and death stalked the citizens of Leningrad. Inside we felt warm, happy, sheltered, temporarily safe from the horrors of the siege.

A loud salvo of artillery fire shook the building, but we smiled at one another. They were our guns, firing from the ships on the Neva, sending our own deadly greetings to the enemy in reply to their New Year's message.

Within minutes the food was gone. I debated with myself whether I ought to bring out the rest of my lake hoard, but decided against it. Shurik and I would have many days when my little reserve might mean the difference between life and death.

"Well, comrades, I must say, it was good," said Commissar Churakov. "May I unbutton my collar?" he asked. "It seems that I have eaten too much and my collar chokes me!"

"But of course," I said. "And you may smoke, too, comrades. As for you, young man, you must go to sleep," I said to Shurik.

"Please, may I stay up a little longer?" he wailed.

"No. But you may stay awake for as long as you wish," said

Dr. Stern, moving to the edge of the sofa and clearing a space for me to prepare Shurik's bed.

Shurik brightened up. "I'll get in at once," he said.

"Good night, Shurik, sweet dreams."

"Speaking of dreams," said Dr. Yakovlev, "I had a dream last night that the war was over and I was walking through a sausage factory. There were miles of sausages, strung like garlands from window to window, and then outside, from tree to tree. I could even smell the sausages. The dream was so real!" We all laughed. For a moment I thought that I, too, could smell the delicious aroma of fat, rosy sausages.

"I can smell them," Shurik announced from his bed.

"What went on while we were at the lake?" I asked, addressing myself to the group in general.

"Well," Dr. Stern began slowly, puffing on his stubborn pipe, "most important of all, we had our first increase in bread rations. That was on Christmas Day, but many people didn't know about it."

"Why? Wasn't it announced on the radio?" asked Zina.

"The radio stopped working," piped Shurik. "For almost two days there was no radio at all. I was so scared. I thought that Germans sneaked into the city and took over the radio station."

"Yes, it was weird," agreed Dr. Yakovlev. "We are so used to hearing the news over the radio or simply listening to the metronome. It means so much to us. And then—suddenly—nothing. Deadly silence. I, too, thought—well, this is the end."

"A lot of people didn't know about the ration increase until they actually came to the stores for their bread," continued Dr. Stern. "Some of them went wild with joy, kissing the bread, fondling it as if it were the most precious thing in the world—which, in a way of course, it is."

"I remember, before the war, I used to go to the Summer

Garden and feed the swans," said Commissar Churakov pensively. "I used to take a loaf of bread and just stand there, feeding it to the swans. To have all this bread now! That's where I was that Sunday when the outbreak of the war was announced."

"And I was at the Medical Institute," said Dr. Stern slowly. "I was to be honored by a group of my graduating students with a special lunch that day."

"I remember!" cried Zina excitedly. "I was among them, and I was in charge of decorating the table. I was arranging flowers when I heard the news on the radio. Where were you, Kyra?" She turned to me.

"I? I was at the theater, in my dressing room. We had closed-circuit radio at the theater to let us know what was on stage. Suddenly it stopped, and the announcement from Moscow was switched on. Half the audience left the theater at once," I said, remembering that fateful day of June twenty-second, six months ago.

"I was playing in the yard with other kids," Shurik broke in, his eyes bright with excitement. "My mother suddenly ran from our flat, grabbed me by the hand and dragged me into our apartment. Then she cried and said that the Germans had attacked our country and that we were at war." Shurik was talking fast, as if afraid that someone might order him to stop talking and go to sleep.

"I remember when we were organized into 'Artistic Brigades' to entertain the troops," I said. "It was in the very first weeks of the war. We had some famous people with us. For instance, the composer Dmitri Shostakovich was our musical director. He worked with us whenever he was free from fireman's duty at the Conservatory of Music. He looked so funny in his uniform!" I smiled, remembering the famous composer in his ill-fitting uniform and bright bronze helmet with a sharp point, shaped like

Kaiser Wilhelm's helmets of World War I.

In October, Shostakovich and many other notables of Leningrad were evacuated. Our "Artistic Brigade" fell apart. I was mobilized for medical training. It felt like it all happened years ago.

"We kids had to paint over the street signs," said Shurik, determined to stay awake. "In case German parachutists landed in the city, we kids had to paint out all the names of streets to confuse them. We were given thick paint and brushes, and we covered all the signs." Shurik obviously enjoyed this memory.

"I'll never forget my *druzhinniza* training," I continued. "I never felt as exhausted as I felt then. All those long hours of crawling on my belly under barbed wire. Or dragging a man on a tarpaulin, and his machine gun behind me—and my gun, too."

Dr. Stern had a wry smile on his face. "You know," he said, "your memories of *druzhinniza* training remind me of something funny. During the first month of the war, we at medical headquarters had the brilliant idea of using special dogs to pull the wounded away from the combat zone. Well, let me tell you, the idea didn't work, for the dogs refused to work under fire. They ran in all directions, leaving the girls to pull the sleds."

"Why, this is exactly what happened on the Road of Life," cried Zina.

"Dogs are smarter than people," said Shurik with conviction. "They don't want any part of war. What kind of dogs were they?"

"German shepherds."

"Now I know!" Shurik cried triumphantly, sitting up in bed. "German shepherds! We should have used Russian shepherds. They wouldn't have run away."

We all broke out in laughter.

Shurik looked at us in bewilderment and then said, "I'd better go to sleep."

"Yes, my boy," said Dr. Stern. "It's getting late. Let's all go now and have a few hours of rest."

I bade good-night to my friends and held the candle high, lighting the way out of my apartment. Then I bolted all the doors and returned to my room. Shurik was already asleep. Not a crumb was left on the table, not a drop of liquor or coffee. It was a good party.

Druzhinnizas, field nurses, marching to their barracks. Note their footgear—there were not enough small-sized boots to outfit thousands of women soldiers. *Wide World Photos*

World-famous composer Dimitri Shostakovich in his fireman's uniform on the roof of the Leningrad Conservatory of Music. *Wide World Photos*

9

All through the night the Germans kept bombarding the city. The shells fell at random, for the enemy wanted all parts of Leningrad to suffer their special holiday message.

Through my sleep I heard the explosions. Once or twice I was aware of the house shaking as the shells fell nearby. I had become so accustomed to the incessant bombardments that I continued to sleep. In the morning we discovered that we had no water even for tea.

"Never mind. We'll have it at the hospital," I said.

The sun was brilliant. The cold air was fresh and invigorating, and if it weren't for the charred buildings around us, I could have said that the city was sparkling.

Although it was still early in the morning, a long queue of women stood in front of the still-locked bakery. We passed them at a brisk pace. I felt a stab of pain as I glanced at them. They looked like the grotesque characters from Goya's etchings. They were skeletons, dressed in layers of clothing and blankets. Their feet were often wrapped in sheets of brown paper, or old rags over their boots and galoshes. They hoped it would protect their feet from frostbite.

But worst of all were the expressions on their faces. I had never seen such expressions of resignation as I saw on the faces of these women, waiting for their daily crumbs of bread. I felt that they were all marked for death.

They huddled by the sides of the building, ignoring a corpse in the middle of the street. The body was fully clothed, except for the *valenki* which had been removed. His bare feet grotesquely protruded from the snow, toes pointing toward the cloudless blue sky. His eyes were open, reminding me of the lusterless eyes of a waxen figure.

"He wasn't here yesterday," Shurik said matter-of-factly. "I went with the girls for water, and he wasn't here."

"Don't look at him," I said.

"I'm not afraid. I never dream of corpses. I dream of good things."

I squeezed his little hand and quickened my steps. Maybe he didn't dream of corpses, but I did.

At the hospital, we found three ambulances unloading. Among the *druzhinnizi* I saw my friend Valya, now fully recovered.

"*Zdoróvo!*" she shouted cheerfully. "This must be your Shurik? The patients say that he is the best thing that has happened to them since the increase in bread rations!"

Shurik smiled shyly, but Valya had already gone.

Inside the hospital the familiar routine was in full progress. Shurik and I changed into our hospital attire, then went our separate ways in pursuit of our tasks.

It was good to be back.

In the afternoon the chief nurse summoned me to her tiny office, a cubicle over the staircase.

She was a jolly middle-aged woman, with frizzly hair which refused to stay under her nurse's cap. She must have been plump once. Now she was thin like the rest of us. Her cheeks hung down, making her resemble a mournful basset hound. Whenever she laughed, the folds of her cheeks jumped up and down, as if they had a life of their own.

Everyone called her Mamma Lisa. The name originated at a staff meeting when she attacked *zavkhoz* Ozerov for not providing enough clean pillowcases.

"You must arrange for better laundry service," she stormed.

The *zavkhoz* just smiled his usual condescending, inscrutable smile.

"Don't you give me this Mona Lisa smile," she exploded. "I need clean linen for my patients and not your charming smiles!"

Ever since then, our chief nurse was Mamma Lisa.

"You asked for me?" I said, knocking at her door.

"Yes, come in. I have an unpleasant job for you. Since you are one of our strongest nurses, due to the good food you had at the lake, I must put you in charge of carrying the dead into the backyard," she said.

"What do I have to do?"

"Just carry the bodies on stretchers into the yard. Twice a week a truck is supposed to come to pick them up. We'll have another girl help you."

"Are there many corpses?" I asked.

"Right now there are seven or eight. The truck didn't come yesterday. By the way," she smiled warmly, and thousands of wrinkles spread over her face, "your Shurik is pure gold. He writes letters for the men, he reads, he draws pictures for them, he feeds them, brings bedpans, walks the men through the corridors—he does everything!"

"I'm glad to hear that he is so useful," I said as I left her office.

I went to the backyard to see the depository for the dead. The bodies, covered with a tarpaulin, were stacked like cordwood against the stone wall. As I was returning to the building, I smelled the peculiar odor of turpentine. I stopped and looked back. A truck backed up into our yard. It was laden with dead bodies, some partially dressed, others swathed in old sheets or blankets, mummy fashion.

The soldiers alighted and swiftly loaded the dead from our yard, holding them by their feet and shoulders, throwing them into the truck like logs into a furnace. The frozen bodies landed with a dull thud.

The soldiers sprinkled turpentine over the ground where the bodies had lain. Then they covered the truck with the tarpaulin and were gone.

"They use turpentine as a disinfectant!" I noted, returning to the hospital. For weeks the city streets had smelled of turpentine. Now I knew why.

I felt very depressed when I resumed my duties at the hospital. In the corridor I met Natasha and Vera, my colleagues from Ladoga. They were chatting excitedly with one another, giggling into their cupped hands in the manner of peasant girls. Apparently Dr. Karpova kept her word and hadn't punished them for illegally possessing butter. It made me feel better to hear them laugh. The contrast between the macabre scene in the yard and these lively girls was typical for Leningrad; it was the contrast between life and death itself.

"Dr. Stern is looking for you," said Natasha to me.

I went straight to the colonel's office. The door was ajar but I knocked.

"Come in, come in, we are waiting for you," said Dr. Stern from behind his desk.

"We are having an emergency senior staff meeting. We have no time to waste," Dr. Stern began. "I have requested the arrest of Lieutenant Ozerov, the director of supplies. He was caught

stealing supplies from the hospital. The investigators are already
here, waiting for him. By now, he may be on his way to the
Internal Security headquarters," the chief continued. "As for the
rest of us, the investigators will call us for questioning one by
one. Don't be alarmed; if you haven't stolen, you have nothing
to worry about," he tried to joke.

"What will happen to the *zavkhoz?*" asked Mamma Lisa.

"He will probably be shot," said the commissar coldly.

A chill ran down my spine. I shivered. Shot! For a few stupid
sausages and a handful of chocolate candies! Shot! But I knew
that in time of war his crime was very serious. Probably he was
stealing lots of food from the hospital, far more than his personal
need demanded. He was, most likely, selling his stolen food on
the black market. People said that one could buy a diamond ring
for a loaf of bread or a whole suite of fine antique furniture for
a few bars of chocolate. One could only imagine what riches our
zavkhoz would possess by trading his stolen food on the black
market. The authorities waged an all-out war against thieves and
speculators. They established special battalions of *Istrebiteli,* "the
destroyers," whose job it was to patrol places where black mar-
keteers gathered and arrest them on the spot. Members of the
Istrebiteli were given authority to inspect bakeries and food shops,
searching for thieves and speculators. There was so little food in
Leningrad that the theft of bread meant certain death for dozens
of people. No wonder that the *Istrebiteli* were fierce and pitiless
in their pursuit of thieves. They instilled fear and hatred in the
hearts of dishonest managers of food shops, because they were
scrupulously honest and idealistic. They were unbribable.

I approved the swift action of the *Istrebiteli* wholeheartedly
which, in most instances, meant death by a firing squad. However,
when someone from our own group was likely to be shot, the

idea made me feel uncomfortable.

"Anyhow, comrades, the crook has been caught," said Commissar Churakov. "Let's not allow this disgusting episode to undermine our dedication to our work."

We all got up and left the office. In the corridor I saw Shurik shuffling from foot to foot, impatiently waiting for me.

"I just saw *zavkhoz* Ozerov in handcuffs!" he whispered excitedly. "What did he do?"

"He stole food from the hospital." I felt that I had to tell the truth.

"They'll shoot him," said Shurik with conviction. "And they'll print it in the *Leningradskaya Pravda*. I saw an article in the paper with the names of all the thieves who were shot." Shurik seemed to be excited about the possibility of seeing Ozerov's name in the paper more than about the reason for such a distinction.

"Run along, I must go to the operating room," I said. He ran downstairs, and I went to the scrub room.

What has happened to me? I thought. I had no pity for a man about to be shot. No pity—only revulsion.

The orderly brought Polivanov in. He was conscious and attempted a wan smile, recognizing Dr. Stern's face behind his surgical mask. Polivanov's legs were unbandaged, ready for examination. They were a frightful sight. His wounds refused to heal. They were still angry red, with the edges turning to a sickly green.

"How am I doing?" he whispered hoarsely, looking at the colonel earnestly.

"Not bad," murmured Dr. Stern, patting his arm reassuringly. "You are getting along just fine!"

I knew he was lying. Polivanov's legs were becoming gangrenous. Despite our efforts, the sergeant was slipping away from us.

Zina administered a strong, intravenous injection to Polivanov. Within moments he was deeply asleep.

"Do you think we'll have to amputate?" she asked, looking at Dr. Stern.

"No!" he said emphatically. "We'll keep trimming the fringes as long as it is possible. It's only the fringes that are gangrenous. Look inside the wound. You'll see that it is red and viable. I will not amputate unless there is no alternative."

It was difficult to bandage his wounds. I had to place several rubber tubes into the wounds to allow for drainage. Hopefully they would work, to prevent further tissue damage.

After Polivanov, there were fifty more soldiers for treatment. When the last patient left the operating room, Dr. Stern raised his arms wearily above his head, stretched and took off his mask.

"Well, I don't know about you, girls, but I'm dead," he declared. "Look at my hands; they shake like leaves." He stretched his hands before us. Indeed they were shaking as if he were palsied.

"I'll try to catch a nap for an hour or so." He removed his gloves and changed his surgical gown to a white hospital coat.

Zina and I went into the wards. Suddenly I heard my name called. I was surprised that someone knew it. Usually we were called by our military rank only, for no one remained in the hospital long enough to know our names.

"Who are you? Do I know you?" I asked the soldier who was smiling broadly.

"Sure you do. I'm Yuri Stepanov. We were in the Artists' Brigade together."

"But of course," I exclaimed. "I didn't recognize you behind these bushes!" I indicated the considerable growth of heavy whiskers around his face.

I looked at his chart. He was wounded at Nevskaya Dubrovka. Shrapnel splinters and a broken arm. Temperature normal. Yuri Stepanov was a famous actor from the Leningrad Theater of Young Spectators, a marvelous theater for children, where a company of specially trained actors performed a repertory written exclusively for the young.

When our brigade was disbanded, I lost track of most of my colleagues. I knew that some of them had been evacuated from Leningrad, while others, like myself, were mobilized for war duties. Yuri was among those who found himself at the front, fighting on the approaches to the city. Now he was wounded and recuperating in our hospital.

"It's good to see you again, Yuri," I said. "I'll be back as soon as I can and we'll chat."

"Fine. Bring me something to read. I'm almost through with this one." He pointed to the bound copy of an old International Literature magazine.

"I'll send Shurik to you. Tell him what you want and he might find it for you. We have a rather good library here." I smiled at him and hurried after Zina, whose scowling face I could see in the doorway.

"Wait till she learns that this is Yuri Stepanov!" I thought, for Russian girls are wild about theater celebrities.

The routine of hospital work, household chores, lugging water and chopping furniture for firewood consumed me. I could think of nothing but the immediate goals of everyday living. I had not read a book in weeks. When I returned home at night—tired, cold and hungry—there was no electricity. To read in the flickering light of a candle was too hard on my eyes. So I listened to the radio, deriving whatever pleasure I could from its excellent programs of music, poetry readings and dramatizations of classics. There were special programs for children. Shurik listened to them avidly.

One morning, during the first week of January, Shurik and I heard a radio announcement that there would be several children's *novogódnyeh yólki,* New Year's holiday parties, to which all the children of Leningrad were invited. Before the war these parties were a yearly tradition. The huge *yólki,* fir trees, decorated with colorful lights and toys, were placed in the halls and gymnasiums of hundreds of Russian schools, theaters and even on the squares of the cities. Tens of thousands of children came to these parties to dance, to see special shows and to receive little gift bags of sweets and fruits.

No one thought this Christmaslike tradition would be continued during the siege. But here was an announcement inviting all the children to participate in the New Year celebration.

"May I go?" Shurik jumped up and down with excitement. "They said the details will be published in the *Leningradskaya Pravda.* Where can we get the paper?"

"Dr. Stern receives it. I'm sure you can look it up in his office."

Shurik could barely wait for us to get to the hospital. He ran up to Dr. Stern's office and knocked on the door.

"I have something very important to tell to you," he said through a keyhole, afraid that Dr. Stern might ask him to come later.

"All right, come in, what is it?" asked Dr. Stern.

"Do you have a copy of *Leningradskaya Pravda?*" queried Shurik, without preliminaries.

"Help yourself. Here it is." He pointed to the copy of the paper lying on his desk. Shurik eagerly snatched the single sheet and searched for the announcement.

"Here it is!" he cried. "There are parties at the Pushkin Theater of Drama, the Maly Opera Theater, and at the Bolshoi Drama Theater! In addition, there are parties for the younger kids at their orphanages." Then his face darkened. "I don't think that I can go," he said wretchedly. "It says here that only kids who live in orphanages may go to these parties."

"But what about the *yólki* at the theaters? Surely you can go there," said Dr. Stern.

"They are for the older kids, from the seventh to the tenth grades." Shurik was crestfallen.

"Nonsense! Let me see." Dr. Stern took the paper and read the announcement.

"I'll telephone the Office of People's Instruction and order a ticket for you," he said. "This is just right—*The Three Musketeers*. It is presented at the Maly Opera Theater, not too far from us. You're going to a party, young man, and there is nothing that can stop you." Shurik ran to the chief, throwing his arms around his neck in the manner of all happy little children. Dr. Stern hugged him tightly for a moment and then released him with a light slap.

"Run along now." Shurik didn't have to be told twice. He dashed out of the office, brimming with joyous excitement.

"Thanks a lot," he yelled from the staircase.

Dr. Stern picked up the paper again; he pointed to an article on the top of the page. The headline said, "Report of the Destroyers' Brigades." I glanced quickly at the contents. So many people were caught stealing food; so many executed. Among the executed, the name OZEROV leaped to my eyes.

I put the paper down. A feeling of nausea overcame me.

Dr. Stern watched me closely. "The investigation proved that our *zavkhoz* was a thief," he said. "Take hold of yourself. What is our schedule for today?"

I handed him the schedule and our day began.

In the afternoon Dr. Stern called me to his office again. I was still working in the wards when Shurik came running to me, a broad, happy smile on his pale face.

"Tomorrow I go to the show! Dr. Stern said that the ticket will be waiting for me at the box office!"

"Wonderful," I said, happy for my boy.

When I finally finished my work Shurik, still at my elbow, followed me to Dr. Stern's office. He was waiting for me.

"I just received a request from headquarters to send one qualified nurse to accompany a large convoy of seriously wounded from the lake," he began, inviting me to sit down. "I don't know why they must be brought into the city now, when we are trying to evacuate everyone. Must be something going on which prohibits the evacuation through Tikhvin."

"Maybe another German offensive," I suggested.

"Maybe. Anyhow, I decided to send you. I know"—he interrupted my gesture of protestation—"I know, you've just returned from there, but I have no choice. You are the strongest right now. I have no alternative but to send you there again."

I knew that it was useless to argue. Military discipline did not permit it anyway, even though Dr. Stern rarely invoked his prerogatives as commanding officer.

"When do I go?" I asked.

"Tomorrow night. You may have a day off. Take Shurik to the theater, then bring him back here."

Shurik listened to the conversation with great attention.

"Does she have to go?" he asked pleadingly.

"I'm sorry, my boy, she must. Fortunately it will be just one convoy. A day or two, no more."

"I'll be ready!" I said, trying to sound nonchalant.

"OK, go home now and rest." We bade him good-by and left.

It was another sunshiny day when we awakened the next morning.

"I don't remember ever seeing so much sunshine in the winter," said Shurik. He blew hard on the windowpane, hoping to thaw out a little peephole with his warm breath.

"Yes, and I don't ever recall such a cold winter," I agreed, fighting with my stove, which refused to light.

My bookcase was long gone, as were most of my books. I had been burning green wood, which produced very little heat even if it did catch fire. Colonel Stern gave me several contraband logs from the hospital supply, which Shurik and I carried home on our little sled. Now I was burning the last pieces. What could I burn next? I looked at my bed. It was one of those large, old-fashioned, heavily built beds, with elaborate carving on the headboard and at the foot. It was made of oak and the wood had a glossy patina of age and innumerable polishings through the years.

I suppose I'll have to start chopping that next, I thought sadly. Destroying my beautiful bed disturbed me, but there was no other choice.

At last the wet wood caught fire. The timid tongues of flame began to lick the thin logs.

"OK, soon we'll have tea. How is the food reserve?"

Shurik opened a suitcase where we kept our provisions. "We still have some ham and sugar."

"Good. I'll bring more food from the lake." Somehow, today, in the bright sunshine, the idea of going back to Ladoga didn't seem to be so dreadful.

Beyond our window the German artillery began methodically shelling the city once again.

"Let's go," I said. "It's no use waiting for the end of this barrage. It might last for the rest of the day. We don't want to be late for your party."

Once on the street we listened for a while, to determine where the shells were exploding. The enemy bombarded us in a systematic pattern so that one could almost predict which side of the street was safest.

"I think the shells are landing on Petrogradskaya Storona," Shurik said, cocking his head like a puppy hearing a familiar whistle.

"Yes, I think you're right. It must be somewhere around Finlandsky Railroad Station. Let's go, I think we're safe now." We trotted toward the Opera House.

At the entrance to the theater there was a large crowd of teenagers and a few children of Shurik's age. They were all pale and thin, bundled in all kinds of winter clothing and shawls, all looking hungry. But they seemed pleased to go to the show, although they behaved like little old men and women. There was no laughter, not the usual horseplay which generally accompanies gatherings of young people. They were pathetically quiet. Only their faces were illuminated by the expectation of a treat. They looked forward to a holiday dinner, after the show— a special dinner, without surrendering their daily ration coupons.

I got Shurik's ticket from the bundled-up cashier at the box office and showed him where to go. In an instant he was swallowed by the crowd. I lost sight of him.

"I'll meet you right here at the end of the show!" I shouted.

Crossing the little park on my way home I noticed a strange person. I couldn't decide whether it was a man or a woman. I couldn't see the face. The person was dressed in a man's fur coat and a woman's wool shawl, with feet wrapped in strips of Persian carpet. In front of this creature stood an artist's easel. Next to the easel there was a child's sled with a large box of paints and a tin container bristling with brushes.

The artist was busy painting the street scene of Leningrad during the siege. On the unfinished canvas I saw the brilliant

blue January sky, the corner of the classic façade of the Philharmonic Hall, the snowdrifts and the inevitable bent figure of
an exhausted citizen, pulling a corpse on a child's sled.

I watched the artist for a few moments and then, quietly, I
went away. For some reason I felt timid, not knowing what to
say to the artist. His painting would haunt my memory forever.

I finished my chores at home and returned for Shurik.

"How was it?" I asked him when I spotted him in the crowd.

"Terrific! They gave us *kasha* and a slice of bread and three
candies." I smiled to myself. I meant, how was the show, but of
course, to Shurik, as to all of us, the food was most important.

"That's wonderful. But did you like the show?"

"Oh, yes, it was very good. When I grow up, I'll be like
d'Artagnan. I'll learn fencing and I'll——"

"OK, OK, let's go. Soon it will be dark, and I must be on my
way to Ladoga." I tugged at his arm as we hurried across the
square.

The artist was gone. The little park was deserted. As we
approached the exit, I noticed a partially broken park bench.
Its narrow wooden planks were torn from its metal frame by
someone, undoubtedly in search of fuel. He was probably too
weak to finish the job or was scared off by a passer-by.

"Do you think we can carry these planks without the sled?"
I asked Shurik. "We have no wood at home."

"We can try," said my boy with a grown man's seriousness.
"If they're too heavy, we can always drop one or two."

I quickly went to work. I struggled with the bench furiously,
afraid that someone might catch me before I was through.

"Watch for militiamen . . . If one comes—yell," I instructed
Shurik over my shoulder.

"One is coming," Shurik cried almost immediately.

It was too late to run. The militiaman saw us and came
straight toward us.

"What are you doing, Comrade Lieutenant! Don't you know that you're destroying government property?" he admonished me severely. He was an elderly man, unshaven and thin. His blue militia coat hung on him, obviously too large. There was no way out for me but to admit the truth. I knew that it was within his power to arrest me for the crime of destruction of government property. The penalty—jail and forced labor and maybe even the firing squad.

"Comrade militiaman, I'm sorry. This bench was already broken. I was going to take these planks home. We have no wood. Please, don't arrest me."

I talked fast, hoping that the militiaman was probably a father himself and would have pity on me, for Shurik's sake.

"Please, *dyádenka,* uncle, don't arrest her," Shurik began to cry, tugging at the man's sleeve. Tears rolled down his thin face, and his voice was full of fear.

The man looked at us for a moment and then said gruffly, "The way you do it, you'll never get the planks loose. Here, let me help you." He grabbed the planks and wrenched them off the frame. "Go away fast now. This bench is no good anyway. If it were not you, someone else would finish it. Go, before someone comes!" He turned away from us to continue on his patrol.

"Thank you, comrade," I said with deep gratitude.

"The bench was no good, anyhow," he repeated, without looking at me. "It's better that the boy be warm."

"Thank you, *dyádenka.*" Shurik wiped his tears, smudging them all over his face.

"Go, quickly," repeated the militiaman.

We didn't need to be told again. We gathered the planks and, dragging them behind us, left the park.

That evening I departed for the Road of Life once again.

10

The warmth of the cab and the monotonous rocking of the ambulance lulled me to sleep. I wasn't aware of the shell-torn road, nor the numerous detours and incessant bombardment. My sleep was deep, as if drugged. When I finally awoke, feeling refreshed, the ambulance had stopped. It was dark outside. I couldn't make out whether we were in the woods or already at the lake.

"Where are we?" I asked the driver.

"In the forest. We're almost at Ladoga, though. There must be a bottleneck ahead. Want to stretch your legs?" He leaned over me and shook the door handle until the door opened.

A wave of cold, fresh air, smelling of pine, rushed into the cab. I breathed deeply and jumped to the ground. In the darkness of the night as far as I could see, there were trucks, ambulances and passenger cars, packed solidly in one long column. The lights of the vehicles illuminated the snowdrifts on the side of the road. From the opposite direction, another long column moved steadily toward Leningrad, their headlights burning with full intensity.

"Don't they camouflage anymore?" I asked the driver.

133

"No use," he said laconically. "If the Fritzes want to shell the road, they do it whether the trucks are lighted or not. But for us, it is easier to drive with lights on."

"But what about the planes?"

"They haven't bombed us from the air for days. Must be short of planes."

I took a few steps off the road and immediately fell through the snow up to my hips.

"You'd better stay on firm ground," advised the driver. "The forest is heavily mined."

I walked up and down the road, afraid to venture too far from the ambulance. Finally the trucks ahead of us began to move. We resumed our journey at a snail's pace.

It was weird to see the convoys moving with their lights turned on in full force. I was so used to the complete darkness of Leningrad that it made me feel uncomfortable to be in the midst of this exposed column.

At Osinovetz, too, I saw an endless ribbon of bright lights, winding across the lake and disappearing in the darkness. Those were the trucks, crossing the lake from Kabona and Novaya Ladoga, toward our shores.

We are getting really bold, I thought.

We stopped before the familiar little log hospital, which I remembered so well from my previous trip.

"Here we are. Do you know where to go?" asked the driver.

"Don't worry, I've been in Osinovetz before. I know my way around here," I said.

We parted company, and I entered the hospital.

An efficient-looking girl in a private's uniform, not more than seventeen, checked my papers.

"You'll be going across the lake at exactly twenty-two hours zero zero minutes," she told me dryly. "You have just enough time for a cup of tea at the communal barracks across the yard."

At ten o'clock exactly, I was back at the hospital. I expected to find a long caravan of sledges. Instead, there were four passenger cars. During my brief absence from the lake it seemed that many improvements had been made. A group of nurses was gathering on the wooden steps. I glanced over them quickly, searching for a familiar face. There was none.

The trip across Ladoga took about two hours. The cars moved swiftly, for there was not much traffic going from Osinovetz. On the other hand, the road leading from the opposite shore was choked with vehicles, moving in one endless stream toward the city. From time to time our headlights would illuminate the huge posters reading "*Voditel*, driver, did you make your two trips today?"

"Do you have a norm for drivers now?" I asked our chauffeur.

"Yes. We must make a minimum of two round trips daily."

That meant four crossings. At their average speed, the drivers must be at the wheel no less than eighteen hours a day.

Kabona was a typical small Russian village. In summer most of the few hundred inhabitants were fishermen, while in winter, they felled trees.

Now the forest stood topless. Artillery shells had shorn the treetops off as if a giant barber had used a huge clipper on their crowns. The village huts were dark behind blackout curtains. But the sounds of barking dogs—sounds I hadn't heard for months—came from the barns and backyards.

On the shore of the lake, as in Osinovetz, stood newly-built warehouses and barracks. Despite the late night hour, the landing bustled with activity. Trucks were loaded, ambulances rolled steadily onward and staff cars darted among them like May bugs.

We were billeted in peasant huts. Our hosts were accustomed for generations to living in crowded conditions, and they didn't mind having us share their little houses.

In my hut only an old woman and nine small children were left. All able men and women were at the front. But Kabona was full of men, nevertheless, for it was the headquarters of one of the supply routes to Leningrad. It was full of refugees, too. Kabona was the first stop on the mainland where evacuees were given hot meals and medical aid.

The village had a boomtown atmosphere. I suppose it was like the vigorous atmosphere of an American gold rush, when a new town would spring to life in a week. Or the discovery of oil in the midst of an Arabian desert, when out of nowhere, hundreds of people would appear, pitching their tents on the hot sands.

There were no hot sands in Kabona, but there were plenty of tents. Road maintenance crews, drivers and antiaircraft garrisons all lived in tents, for the village houses couldn't accommodate any more people.

I woke up next morning, and for a few moments I was disoriented. Then I had a strange feeling that I was being watched. I sat up and looked around. Indeed I was being watched. There were four or five little children peeking at me through a half-opened door. When they realized that they were discovered, they scattered, giggling and shoving.

It was a great pleasure to hear children's laughter. Other than Shurik, I hadn't seen a child for weeks. An old woman came into my room.

"A soldier is waiting for you," she announced. "He wants you to go with him to the hospital at once. Hurry."

As I rushed through the front room, buckling my gun belt around my waist, I saw a cluster of youngsters scattering in all directions, like little colorful bugs.

I'll make friends with them yet, I thought. The prospect of playing with them made me feel warm and happy.

I hurried after the guide. He led me to a string of freight cars standing on a railroad siding. On each car there was a red cross emblem hastily marked in chalk. On the snow in front of the cars stood field kitchens surrounded by vaporous clouds of steam. The delicious aroma of meat stew made my empty stomach contract. Young women cooks, dressed in shortened camouflage robes, bustled about the kitchens.

"This is the medical staff headquarters." The soldier pointed. "Report there." He left, without saluting.

I climbed the few steps of the iron ladder leading into the car. It was very warm and stuffy inside. The portable iron stove emitted lots of heat, and people, working at the desks, were all in shirt-sleeves.

"Are you a nurse from the group that arrived last night?" a tall man in a major's uniform asked me. "I am Dr. Kostrov, the commanding officer. You are ordered to remain in Kabona indefinitely, or until we get a replacement."

Indefinitely! I thought angrily. I wished there were a way to disobey. I was furious at the prospect of having to stay on. I felt that I had been tricked into this tour of duty. I was supposed to be away from home only for a day or two!

"You are assigned to car four. Regular ward duty," continued Dr. Kostrov, ignoring my angry look.

"But I am a surgical nurse," I protested. "I am a deputy charge nurse at my hospital." The idea of being a plain ward nurse didn't appeal to me.

Dr. Kostrov looked at me intensely. He probably detected a note of rebellion in my voice.

"Oh, you are? So much the better. We'll call on you when we need you. Dismissed!" There was no use arguing.

Car four, where I was to commence my duties, was lined with broad shelves on which the wounded lay five or six in a row. In

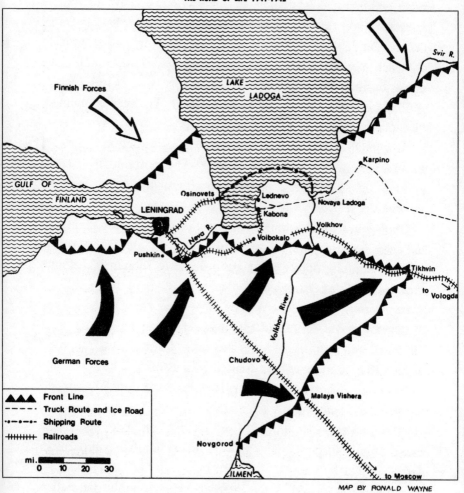

THE ROAD OF LIFE 1941-1942

Svir R.

Finnish Forces

LAKE LADOGA

Karpino

GULF OF FINLAND

Osinovets
Lednevo
LENINGRAD
Kabona
Novaya Ladoga
Neva R.
Volkhov
Voibokalo
Pushkin
Tikhvin
to Vologda

German Forces

Volkhov River

Chudovo

Malaya Vishera

Novgorod

ILMEN

to Moscow

Front Line
Truck Route and Ice Road
Shipping Route
Railroads

mi.
0   10   20   30

MAP BY RONALD WAYNE

the center stood a sizable iron stove, almost pink from the constantly raging fire inside.

The wounded, covered only with gray hospital blankets, seemed to be of good cheer. None seemed to be a serious case.

"Hey, we got a new nurse!" yelled one of them, closest to the door.

"Let's get acquainted, comrades," I said. "As I read your names, please reply so that I may associate your face with your name. As you can see, without your chart hanging at the foot of your bed, it is difficult to know who's who."

"It's difficult without beds, too," joked one of the soldiers, and we all laughed.

I'll be OK here, I thought.

It was amazing how fast time passed in Kabona! Two weeks had slipped away, unnoticed. I became fast friends with the children. They always waited for my return from the hospital, sometimes falling asleep at the table while waiting. The younger children sat on my lap, two at a time, while the older ones fought for the privilege of sitting next to me or carrying my medical bag into my room. I found myself sharing sweets with them—the sweets I had so jealously collected to take home to Shurik.

On January twenty-fourth, I was told that food rations in Leningrad had been increased again. I felt triumphant. I saw for myself how much food accumulated in Kabona for shipment to Leningrad. I witnessed the heroic attempts of the drivers in delivering it to the city. Now I felt assured that, despite enemy efforts to prevent it, food was reaching the starving Leningraders.

Here, in Kabona, we had no shortages. I was able to save plenty of canned meat, fish and chocolate. And since I didn't smoke, I saved all my cigarette rations. They were as good as bread for barter in Leningrad.

February arrived, but I was still in Kabona. I missed Shurik and my friends at the hospital. I kept writing to Dr. Stern, asking him to put pressure on headquarters and have me reassigned to the city, but to no avail.

In mid-February the new railroad branch Voibokalo-Kabona was finished. Now supplies from the mainland could be brought directly to the lake shore for reloading on trucks.

An air of jubilation spread over the soldiers, workers, drivers and the few remaining citizens of Kabona. Despite the efforts of the enemy, we had succeeded in building a railroad, right under their noses.

To celebrate the occasion, all the 19,000 people working on the supply routes were issued an additional ration of vodka. Children were given little parcels of sweets, but only the youngest ones eagerly accepted them. Older children, instead, collected the sweets, crated and sent them on to the "Heroic Children of Leningrad."

That night, after celebrating with my patients the opening of the new railroad, I saw a beautiful Husky sniffing around my hospital car. It was a fluffy, friendly dog, obviously used to being around people.

The moment the Husky saw me, it picked up something which looked like an old muff. It was a puppy! The Husky wagged her tail and ran to me. I took the puppy from her. It was cuddly and warm, and its eyes were already opened. It must have been four or five weeks old. I brought it into the car.

"See what I found," I announced to the wounded. They all wanted to pet the animal. They passed the puppy from person to person, petting it, scratching its ears and rubbing noses with it.

There was another bark.

"Not again!" I said. Sure enough, there stood my friend with another puppy in her mouth.

"Here is another one! What shall we do with them?" I asked the soldiers.

"Keep them, of course," they all yelled.

"All right, let me find a box for them, and we'll keep them here. As long as the mother is nursing them, the pups will be all right," I said. "But what will become of them later?"

"Oh, don't worry. Someone will take a pup to his unit when he leaves the hospital. Sort of a mascot," said one of the soldiers.

I put the pups into the box. The mother immediately jumped in, and the pups began to nurse.

I told the children about my new family at the hospital train. They besieged their grandmother, begging to let them have a puppy.

The following evening, with her permission, I brought home one of the pups. I watched the children playing with it, thinking how happy Shurik would be if he had a puppy like that.

February proved to be the month of blizzards. Every day the vicious winds swept over the lake, covering the ice road with towering snowdrifts. Many trucks were stuck in the snow, making the work of the drivers and maintenance crews even more difficult. Everyone cursed the weather. The only benefit from the blizzards was the virtual halt in German air attacks. Their planes were grounded. However, the long-range artillery activities were intensified. Not an hour passed without German shells exploding somewhere along the ice route.

Toward the end of the month, I finally received my orders to return to Leningrad. I bade good-by to my superiors at headquarters—people I had never come to know. Then I said my farewells to my patients.

"Take care of the dogs," I begged them.

"I'll take the mother dog. She's already housebroken. I'm going back to my unit tomorrow," said one of the soldiers.

I was disappointed. I hoped to find a good master for the remaining puppy.

"Why don't you take the pup yourself?" suggested the man. "You told us about Shurik. He would love a dog."

"You must be joking. I can't take a dog into a city, where people are starving!"

"He won't eat much. He is still a puppy."

"Sure. But he won't be a puppy forever." The soldiers laughed.

"No, I'm serious," insisted the patient. "The rations in Leningrad will continue to increase from now on. And think of the joy he will bring Shurik."

"Yes, and work for me." But I already began to waver. Actually, I was sure that this idea was in the back of my mind all the time. I only needed a bit of prodding to induce me to do this utterly crazy thing—taking the dog with me.

"All right, comrades, I shall take the pup," I said to them. "It will remind me of you and Kabona!"

"Call her *Snezhinka*," suggested the soldier, whose idea I was following now so optimistically.

"It's a good name! She does look like a snowflake, so white and fluffy! So, it will be *Snezhinka*." I was delighted with the name.

"Be careful that no one steals the pup. You know how people are in Leningrad. They eat anything—dogs, cats, rats. Anything with meat on it," remarked one of the soldiers with a cruel smile.

I decided not to acknowledge his remark. Instead, I picked up the puppy, and taking her chunky paw, waved good-by with it to the wounded. "See you after the war, in Leningrad." I tucked the puppy inside my coat and asked the soldiers to keep the mother dog in for a while.

"I don't want her to follow me," I explained. "So long!"

My leave-taking from the old woman and the children was more difficult. The children cried. The old *babushka* hung a copper cross around my neck.

"It will protect you from harm," she told me. "If only my daughter wore it, she would have been alive today. But she was killed in an air raid, leaving an old woman with all these children." They all came to the warehouses to see me off. They helped me carry a large bag of food supplies, which I was able to save during my six weeks on the mainland.

I kissed and hugged them all.

The staff car driver honked impatiently. He was to take me straight to my hospital in Leningrad, and he wanted to be on his way. Although the sun was trying to break through the clouds, one was never sure on the lake whether another blizzard wasn't about to unleash its fury on the ice road. The driver helped me store my food reserves in the trunk of his car, and we were off.

I looked back. On the high landing platform stood ten bundled-up little figures, looking like *Matryoshki,* the carved wooden dolls, which progressively diminished in size. The old *babushka* and her nine orphans.

"Are they your folks?" the driver asked as we left the landing.

"No. But I feel as if they were." I unbuttoned my coat and let Snezhinka stick her little head out.

"What have you there—a dog?" cried the driver in disbelief. "I haven't seen a dog since——since I don't remember when."

"I know. I'm bringing her home to my little boy." I stroked the puppy's head, and she caught my fingers with her sharp little teeth.

We rode, following the route well marked with little colorful flags. How familiar was this landscape. How many times had I gone into its whiteness on my skis!

I could see the long strings of convoys on both sides of our road, all moving steadily toward the city. Some of them seen from a distance had an over-all pinkish color. They were trucks carrying frozen carcasses of meat. The others were black. They carried coal. Still others were white, almost dissolving in the whiteness of the landscape. Those were bringing in sacks of flour.

The cargo was no longer camouflaged. Undoubtedly this method of transporting supplies helped to expedite the loading and unloading procedures.

I saw a patrol of two girls on skis, their arm bands proclaiming them to be members of the medical corps. Within two hours we were in Osinovetz. After a short stop for a bowl of soup, which I shared with Snezhinka, we were on the highway to Leningrad.

Ski patrol on the Road of Life. *Wide World Photos*

11

Despite the third increase in food rations during my absence from Leningrad, people continued to die. Their starvation was too far advanced for them to be saved by increases in rations. During December and January mostly men were dying. Now women began to catch up. The known deaths for the first two months of 1942 were 200,000. Some people thought this estimate was too low.

To bury this astronomical number of corpses, the army sappers were ordered into Leningrad. On the outskirts of the city long trenches were dug into which the dead were thrown without count. Or they burned mounds of piled-up bodies in huge bonfires.

I felt devastated as I thought of what this blockade was doing to my people and to my city. Would we ever be able to regain our humanity toward one another and be able to heal the scars of this horrible winter—those of us who might survive?

As we rode into the outskirts of the city, I saw many wooden houses being demolished. The inevitable groups of women and girls worked with crowbars, prying wooden boards off the façades of the small houses.

"Is it permissible now to destroy government property?" I asked the driver, with a touch of sarcasm.

"Indeed it is. An order of the city government was issued a couple of weeks ago, to demolish all wooden structures for use as fuel."

"Good, then I might not need to chop my bed to feed my stove," I said.

"No, I'm afraid you still will have to chop your bed. The wood from the houses is allocated to industry and bakeries."

We rode slowly along the slippery, uneven streets. One could not distinguish any longer between the sidewalk and the road. The whole surface of the street was covered with three to four feet of snow and ice, untouched by cleaning crews for months. The car kept skidding dangerously, causing the driver to swear under his breath.

Slowly we progressed to the center of the city. But even there, the conditions of the streets were no better.

"What a job it will be to clean up the city," the driver said. "I'm glad I am not a woman. It will be the women who will have to do the dirty job." I had to agree that he was probably right.

I didn't stop at my house. As we passed it in the car, I saw that it was still there. My windows were intact behind the strips of paper which I pasted on the glass in crisscross design, to protect them from shattering.

I felt very apprehensive about bringing Snezhinka into the hospital. I knew I would be asking for Dr. Stern's displeasure. *I should have left Snezhinka at home,* I thought. But it was too late. The driver already had stopped the car at the entrance to the hospital. He took my supplies out of the trunk and then stood watching the puppy as she sniffed and pranced about on the snow. I hoped the little dog would be on her best behavior when she met the chief.

"Good-by, Comrade driver," I said, shaking hands with him.

I tucked the dog back inside my coat and picked up the heavy bag with provisions. Then I ran up the few steps leading to the hospital.

Dr. Stern was alone in his office, eating a bowl of soup and reading the paper. His door was partly opened, and as I knocked, I heard his gruff voice from behind the paper. "Come in."

I entered and stood there, waiting for him to lower his paper.

"Kyra!" He stood up and opened his arms wide. I fell into his arms and kissed him on his stubbly, sunken cheek.

"Sit down, sit down, right here. Take your coat off!" He moved a chair for me, almost knocking the unfinished soup off his desk.

I unbuttoned my coat. Snezhinka popped her fluffy head out. It was too late to prepare Dr. Stern. He saw the dog.

"What have you there, a dog? A real, live dog?" He took Snezhinka from my arms and began stroking her soft fur. "What a beautiful puppy. Shurik will love it."

I was astounded by his warm reception of the dog. I expected to be chided, ridiculed or even be ordered to dispose of the dog at once. Instead, Dr. Stern petted the animal, anticipating Shurik's pleasure.

"What's his name?"

"Snezhinka. It's a girl."

"Snezhinka! What a good name for her. Are you hungry, Snezhinka?" He placed his unfinished bowl of soup on the floor and put the puppy down. Snezhinka immediately began to lap the soup up, making a mess around the bowl.

"You are not angry with me?" I asked, still unable to believe my good fortune.

"Angry? No. While it is against the rules, of course, to have pets in the hospital. I think this little dog will do as much good for our morale here as Shurik has done." He continued, wiping the puppy's muzzle with his handkerchief, saying, "This little creature will bring to the soldiers memories of their childhood, the feeling of peacetime. No, I'm not angry with you. I'm glad that you brought Snezhinka to us."

"And you don't believe that it was presumptuous of me to assume that we can feed a dog when people are starving?" I insisted.

"No. We have more than 700 patients here and close to 100 personnel. We can find enough for the puppy among all these hundreds of people. Of course, the dog will grow, but let's be optimistic and hope that our rations will continue to be increased!"

I felt relieved. Now I could face Shurik without the fear of having to give up the little dog later on.

"Well, I think that you're anxious to see Shurik," said Dr. Stern, lighting his pipe. "Let me call him in." The colonel pressed a button on the little electric panel on his desk.

"What? We have electricity now? How marvelous!"

"Yes, we have been provided with a few hours of electricity. The army supplied us with our own generator."

"I can see that a lot of things have changed during these six weeks!"

"Yes, my dear, and all for the best. We have more bread now, and we even get sugar and butter. And meat, too. By we, I mean all the people of Leningrad, not just the military." He sat in his chair, stroking Snezhinka's head. She was sound asleep on his lap, her little belly full of the doctor's dinner.

"How much bread do we get now?" I asked.

"Quite a lot. Workers—500 grams; civilians—350 grams, and children—300 grams. Quite a difference from November, eh?"

"Yes. It means that Shurik and I, together, will be getting exactly two loaves of bread a day. Quite a lot."

I heard the sound of running feet, and presently there was a knock on the door.

"It's Shurik," said Dr. Stern. "Come in, Shurik."

He entered and for a moment didn't see me.

"Look who's here," said Dr. Stern. Shurik turned around and then recognized me.

"Kyra!" he cried, rushing at me with the force of a football player.

I embraced and kissed him, pricking my lips on the growing bristles of his shaven head.

We looked at each other with utter happiness.

"Look at what Kyra brought for you," said Dr. Stern, pointing to the sleeping animal on his lap.

Shurik approached the dog cautiously. "Is it real?" he asked.

Shurik touched Snezhinka's head, and she opened her eyes.

"It's real," he whispered, as if afraid that the wonderful thing he saw would disappear.

"She is real and she is yours," I said to him. "Her name is Snezhinka."

We watched him as he awkwardly held the puppy, afraid to drop her. Snezhinka stuck her quick pink tongue out and licked Shurik's face.

"She likes me," he beamed. "I'll never leave her alone," he said with a solemn expression. "I will be with her all the time, or someone might steal her and sell her for meat."

Dr. Stern cleared his throat loudly, as was his habit whenever he was emotionally upset.

"It seems that Shurik knows much about what's going on in the city. Where do you suppose he gets his information?" he asked rhetorically.

"In the kitchen. The cook and the girls say that one can buy anything on the black market. Any kind of meat—dog meat, cat meat, rats and even human meat!" Shurik's eyes rounded in horror.

"I can't believe it," I said. "Not human flesh!"

"Oh, yes, they say that there is plenty of it on the market. And it looks like veal."

Dr. Stern just shook his head. "There are, indeed, all kinds of ugly rumors about cannibalism. I think, in certain isolated instances, it probably does exist. But you'll be absolutely right in wanting to guard your dog." He turned to Shurik.

"I'll take her to make friends with the cook. He'll save some bones for her," said Shurik.

"Smart boy!" Dr. Stern opened the door for him, and Shurik left, carrying Snezhinka in his arms, beaming with happiness.

"Now, brief me on the situation in Kabona and on the lake." The colonel went back to his seat behind the desk and invited me to take my place opposite him.

Shurik took his new responsibility very seriously. We persuaded Dr. Stern to keep his office door closed so that Snezhinka wouldn't stray. Shurik took the dog into the yard several times a day, and within a week we noticed certain improvements in her training. Everyone was mad about the puppy. Even Zina, after the first few moments of disapproval, had to agree that the presence of the little animal in the hospital lifted the spirits of the wounded. I didn't need to have worried about supporting the dog on our rations. Snezhinka was the fattest, the best fed member of our entire medical establishment. Everyone shared his food with her, and the little glutton had to be watched not to overeat.

Shurik and I took the dog for a walk along the canal every night. We must have presented a rather curious tableau: an armed officer and a child standing guard over a little dog performing its natural functions. But there was no one to enjoy this tableau or to laugh at it. The city looked like a deserted charnel house.

I found that a great change had occurred in Zina during the weeks of my absence. She seemed to be more open, more friendly with the people at the hospital. I remarked about it to our chief.

"I agree with you," he said. "I am sure that our good colleague is in love."

I could hardly wait to get Zina alone. "Dr. Stern tells me that you are in love," I said without preliminaries.

She laughed, that embarrassed little laughter which people use when they are stalling for time.

"Who is it?" I insisted, sounding like a Spanish inquisitor.

"Yuri. Yuri Stepanov."

"Yuri Stepanov! I don't believe it!"

"Why not?" she demanded defensively.

"I mean . . . he is an actor. And you are always so serious, so deeply engrossed in your work and——" I really didn't know what to say, so I just stopped talking.

"He is a fine man. And a very good actor! I have never met anyone before who is so interesting to talk to. He is a very intelligent man," she concluded with pride.

"I know him very little," I said. "I just worked with him a few weeks. Is he still at the hospital?"

"No, no. He was discharged at the end of January. But he comes here often. You see, Yuri's arm is badly injured. I give him physiotherapy and maybe it will help eventually. They assigned him to the Red Army Club as a director of artistic propaganda."

"When is the wedding?" I asked.

"We thought in June, when the weather is warm."

"I'm very, very happy for you, and I think that Yuri is a lucky fellow." I was glad, indeed, that my friend was in love. I was glad for her and a bit envious that I, myself, was not.

I was surprised to see that Polivanov was still in the hospital. I expected to find him either dead or discharged, with both legs amputated. And here he was still with us and still with both his legs.

"It's a long story and a lucky one, too," Dr. Stern told me when I asked him about Polivanov. "After you left for Kabona, we thought that we might have to amputate. The poor man developed thrombophlebitis. Do you know what it is?"

"Yes, I think so. It is when the infection produces blood clots, which can travel through the blood stream."

"Right. This phlebitis triggered an embolism in both of his lungs. For a while, we had not only a badly wounded man, but a very sick man. Now, thank God, he is getting better. It will be a long, slow process of recovery, but if nothing goes wrong, our Polivanov will be well in two or three months, I should say.

"Go and talk to him. We put him in a private room so that we can keep him warm."

I went to see Polivanov. The tiny room, which once was a janitor's walk-in closet, was very warm. There was enough space for only a bed, one chair and a small table on which stood the little tin stove propped on four bricks. But the walls of this windowless room were covered with colorful pictures. I recognized Shurik's art. The artist, himself, was sitting on the chair, reading *Leningradskaya Pravda* aloud to the patient.

"How do you feel, comrade Polivanov?" I asked, checking his chart at the foot of the bed. He still had fever, although I could see that there were days when his temperature was normal.

He smiled wanly at me. He was propped high to an almost sitting position. I knew that if he were to lie down, he might choke from coughing.

"Not too bad, lieutenant. They saved my legs for me." He

pointed to his legs, still heavily bandaged, looking like two thick white logs.

"Yes, I know. Colonel Stern told me about the fight with gangrene. He is a wonderful doctor."

"Good to see you back, lieutenant. Shurik, here, kept telling me about you. I feel that I know you very well. You must be a fine girl." I was embarrassed by his compliment, but it pleased me that Shurik spoke well of me.

"I see that Shurik decorated your room," I said, changing the subject.

"Yes, I don't know what I would have done without him. He became my personal nurse. He reads to me, he feeds me, he talks to me. And he listens to me, which must be very hard for a lad of his age, for I talk a lot." He laughed, but his laughter turned into a cough. He grasped his chest as he coughed, and I could see that he was in pain.

Shurik, with dexterity which surprised me, filled a glass with warm water from the teapot on the top of the stove and held it for Polivanov to drink. Little by little the cough subsided, and Polivanov closed his eyes, utterly exhausted.

"See what I mean about Shurik?" he whispered. "This lad knows by instinct just what to do."

"It is not by my instinct," Shurik objected, as if he were slighted. "Dr. Stern told me what to do. He said each time when you cough, give you warm water to drink. Never cold, only warm. That's why I always keep a teapot on the stove."

"That's why I say that you are going to be a perfect male nurse someday," said Polivanov in a coarse voice, still weak from his paroxysm of coughing.

"I'll be a doctor when I grow up," announced Shurik.

"Oh? I thought that you were going to learn how to fence and be like d'Artagnan," I said.

"That was before I had a talk with Dr. Stern," solemnly

proclaimed Shurik. "He thinks that I have the making of a good doctor. He told me so himself."

"Then a doctor you'll be," Polivanov said with resolution. He was tired. He closed his eyes.

I tugged at Shurik's sleeve and pointed with my eyes to the door. He understood, and we left Polivanov's room, quietly closing the door behind us.

That evening, after the staff meeting, Dr. Stern asked me to remain in his office. He read me a letter, concerning Shurik. It came from the commanding officer of a tank battalion where Shurik's father served as a gunner. In a few, hastily written words, the commander told us that Sergeant Nikanorov was killed in action during the November offensive, near Tikhvin. He apologized for not answering our requests for information earlier, saying that his battalion was constantly on the move.

"What shall we do now?" I asked Dr. Stern. "Shall we tell it to him?"

"I suppose, we should," he replied after a moment of hesitation. "Besides, we'll have to think of evacuating him from the city. He ought to be going to school."

"I can't part with him. Maybe I can adopt him legally now, since he is an orphan?" I looked at Dr. Stern pleadingly, as if it were up to him to grant my wish.

"I don't think that you—a young, unmarried girl—would be considered eligible as an adoptive parent. It's against the law."

I was crestfallen.

There was a buzz on the intercom panel. He picked up his local telephone. "It's Mamma Lisa. She wants you to take a dead body to the courtyard."

I sighed and went to fetch my helper, Natasha. My absence of six weeks didn't relieve me from this loathsome duty.

12

March arrived, and with it the first massive attempt to clean up the city. The government issued an edict that International Women's Day on the eighth of March would be celebrated by a mass turnout of all able women and children for clean-up duty. Shurik and I were assigned to a stretch of the Moika River embankment behind the Mariinsky Opera Theater.

On that day we awoke earlier than usual. We hurried through our breakfast, for we had a long walk ahead of us. I dreaded this new hardship—shoveling snow and chopping ice. Fortunately Dr. Stern arranged that I work for only two hours. He needed me at the hospital.

It was just past dawn when we left our home. The sky looked frosty and pale green. On the horizon it was tinted with rose, like a ripening *Antónovka* apple. The air-defense balloons slowly descended, like huge, lazy silver fish, their job of protecting the city done for another night. The full-throated boom of heavy artillery continued from the distance. Shurik and I paid no attention. This was a part of our life now.

The opera theater looked drab and shabby. Some of its windows were broken. Others were boarded up with plywood. The paint on the classical façade was peeling off, and the snowdrifts piled up against the doors. The goddesses and the muses which decorated the theater had high *shapki* of snow on their heads ever since the first storm in early November.

How well I knew this theater! How often I went there as a very young girl when I was a member of its famed children's choir. How proud I was to show my special pass to the imposing door-man at the artists' entrance. Now it stood cold, empty and silent, its artists evacuated or fighting at the Leningrad Front. Only a token group of technicians remained, working at the set-building shops on special assignment for the city defense headquarters.

I remembered I was greatly astonished when early in the blockade I heard that the set-building shops were making artillery guns and tanks. It sounded incredible, until I learned that they were made of plywood and canvas, meant to confuse the enemy's reconnaissance planes into supposing that we had much stronger defenses than we actually did have.

Behind the theater, in the loading section facing the river, Shurik and I saw several of these discarded "guns" and "tanks." They were crudely made and painted, and we wondered how they could have possibly deceived anyone. However, from the air, they must have looked realistic, particularly interspersed with real artillery guns and tanks.

All around us were women and children. They moved slowly for, without exception, they were malnourished and weak. I couldn't visualize how the city could be cleaned by such crews as ours. But then, there is strength in numbers. There were tens of thousands of people like us, chopping, digging, scraping, clearing tiny patches in the over-all chaos of snow and ice.

As soon as any amount of debris was loosened, we carried it on a flat sheet of plywood to the embankment and dumped it in the river. Eventually the debris would go under with the melting ice. The filth of our waterways when the ice melts would be staggering. But that was something to face later. Now we had to liberate our streets from the millions of cubic feet of frozen snow, dirt and refuse.

Our two hours with a crowbar passed very fast. I secured the signature of our leader, indicating that the work assignment was fulfilled satisfactorily. Shurik and I then departed. We had a full day ahead of us at the hospital.

We crossed the theater square, toward the Leningrad Conservatory of Music. Behind it was Griboyedov Canal, where similar groups of women were piling up heaps of frozen refuse. They had a different system, though. They formed a human chain and passed buckets of dirt and snow from hand to hand to be emptied onto the ice of the canal.

"It reminds me of the chain brigades we formed when there was no water for the bakeries," said Shurik. "You were in Kabona at that time."

"What happened?"

"Well, the water pipes of the bakery were frozen, and they burst. And the bakers couldn't make bread without water. So the city defense council ordered several thousand *Komsomol* members to carry water to the plant. Natasha and Tanya from our hospital had to go there. They asked Dr. Stern if I could go with them. I wanted to help. So Dr. Stern said, 'Fine, Shurik needs fresh air. Take him with you, but see that nothing happens to him.' And I went with them."

"And then what?" I prompted.

"Well, there were many, many young people, school kids, who formed a chain several blocks long. We passed buckets of water from one to another right from the holes in the ice on the Neva. The younger kids were in the second chain, passing the empty buckets back to the holes. It was fun at first, but then my arms

began to ache, and I began to cry. A fellow *Komsomol* saw me
and said, 'Stop working, boy, and go home; you have done enough
for today.' So I went home to the hospital. I couldn't find
Natasha and Tanya, but they looked for me everywhere, and
they were afraid to go back to the hospital. They didn't come
back until dark. They thought that they had lost me."

I listened to his story, seeing in my mind's eye the long chain
of youngsters, passing the heavy buckets of murky water from
one to another so that the bakery wouldn't have to stop its operations and thus condemn to death tens of thousands of citizens.
And Shurik, a true son of Leningrad, among them.

Each day now one could see thousands of women slowly
digging our city out of its dirt. Underneath the layers of filth,
the clean-up brigades kept uncovering hundreds of frozen corpses.
Those were the unfortunates who happened to be on the street
when death overtook them.

The city government, fearing epidemics, ordered mass inoculation of citizens against typhus, typhoid, paratyphoid, cholera,
plague and smallpox. Special vaccines were flown from Moscow
with medical personnel to administer them. Every hospital, public
building and school was converted to an inoculation station. Those
who were too weak to walk to them were inoculated at their
homes by visiting nurses.

Somehow, the whole atmosphere of life in the besieged city
was changing. Death, which brazenly stalked the streets of Leningrad during the winter, still lurked in corners. But now there was
a new hope. Spring was in the air.

Our curfew hour came later. One didn't have to be off the
streets by ten any longer. Now the final hour was eleven. As the
days grew longer, the city cleaner and the increase in rations was
maintained, people began to hope, timidly at first, that maybe
the worst was over. Just maybe.

Then a disaster struck our hospital.

Leningrad hospital set on fire by enemy bombs. *National Archives*

Shipment of wounded soldiers from the front lines. *National Archives*

Leningrad streetcar suffers a direct hit by an enemy long range shell. *Wide World Photos*

Druzhinniza at work. Note her submachine gun. *Wide World Photos*

On the fourth of April, after three months of absence from our skies, the Nazis renewed their air attacks on the city. From the moment we heard the sirens wailing, we knew that we were in for a new trial of endurance.

The planes came in several concentrated waves, dropping huge demolition bombs, followed by a rain of smaller, incendiary ones. They were obviously bent on total destruction of as many buildings as possible.

Shurik and I were just getting up in the morning when the first air raid began.

Fortunately the "all clear" signal sounded shortly, and we, with Snezhinka at our side, quickly walked to the hospital.

There was no one on the street, except for militia patrols. We walked along the sidewalk, cleared of dirt and snow. It was incredible how the women of Leningrad were able to scrape the city clean. There were still huge, two-story-high mounds of melting dirty snow and refuse piled up in the middle of the streets, but the sidewalks looked clean and dry under the first rays of the spring sun.

The porous gray ice on the Griboyedov Canal was cracking under the weight of tons of refuse dumped onto it. Murky black water seeped through the cracks. *A few more sunny days and the dirty snow will disappear forever,* I thought.

We all waited for spring with painful longing. Gone would be the endless, dark nights and cold, grim days. Gone would be the frozen walls of our rooms, the layers of clothing, which failed to keep us warm. Gone, gone would be the horrible, incredible winter, when a million people had perished. Whatever might lie ahead of us, it could never be worse than the winter of 1941–42 in Leningrad!

Shurik was chatting about Polivanov.

"He reminds me a lot of my father."

I glanced at him quickly, but Shurik's face was open, his eyes clear of sorrow, and innocent of the knowledge of his father's death.

We must tell it to him somehow, I thought. *We can't withhold the truth from him forever.*

"*Dyádya* Kolya, uncle Kolya, has two kids," Shurik continued to inform me about Nikolai Polivanov. "He has a boy my age and a younger girl. And he has his own grandmother, still living. Imagine, he, a grown man, has a grandmother."

Snezhinka hearing the gay intonation, leaped up in happy exuberance, trying to snatch a glove from Shurik's hand. They ran ahead of me, carefree, happy young animals. One didn't know who was on the leash, the dog or the boy.

As we reached the hospital, the penetrating wail of sirens announced the approach of another air raid.

"Get in, quick!" I pushed Shurik into the doorway. He scooped up his dog, and we closed the massive doors behind us.

It was my day to be on fire watch. Without changing my clothes, I stuck a bronze fire helmet on my head and prepared to climb the narrow staircase leading to the roof, when Dr. Stern intercepted me.

"I need you in the surgery at once. Hurry up!"

In the nurses' quarters I changed into my hospital uniform. It was no longer necessary to wear a padded jacket under it. For two weeks now we had regular steam heat in the hospital, for the army engineers had repaired our heating system and had thawed out the main water pipe. We still had to go outside to draw water from the open main, but at least our trips to the river were not necessary.

The ice was very treacherous now. It was weakened by hundreds of thousands of tons of snow and refuse scraped from the streets. The arrival of the first warm days of spring made it very dangerous to venture upon the thawing river.

I was glad of it. Soon, the sun would thaw out all the pipes in the city. Once again we would have running water and functioning toilets like civilized people.

Dr. Stern, Zina and Dr. Yakovlev were working at their respective tables, surrounded by nurses. I took my place next to the chief. Beyond the windows the nervous rapid stutter of antiaircraft guns increased. The planes must have reached our locality. They seemed to be right over our roof. Almost instantly there was a whistling sound, growing in intensity. Then a terrible, clashing, thundering impact. There was a loud explosion and the building shuddered violently. The electricity went off, and the windows blew out from the force of the air wave, breaking into millions of sharp splinters. An acrid smell of smoke and brick dust spread through the room.

"Fire!" someone yelled hysterically from behind the closed door of the operating room.

Dr. Stern tore his surgical mask off. "Dr. Karpova and her nurse remain here," he ordered sharply. "Dr. Yakovlev and the rest—come with me." He rushed to the door, but it was jammed. From behind it came the screams of running people and the sounds of growing panic.

"Damn it. We must open this door," shouted Dr. Stern as we all tried to push the heavy oak door open.

"The balcony. The windows must be blown out all along the façade. We can get to the next room from the balcony," cried Dr. Yakovlev, running toward it. He climbed out of the window and shouted from the balcony, "Yes, we can get out. Hurry!" We followed him, leaving Zina and her nurse to finish the work with three already anesthetized patients in the operating room.

In the corridor a human wall, pushing, shoving, fighting, met us and pinned us to the door. The wounded, in one great mass, stampeded toward the staircase leading to the shelter. Their faces were contorted with fear, their mouths open, shouting, their eyes bulging. They hit one another in the faces, fighting every inch of the way to the safety of the shelter.

It was horrible, this torrent of obsessed men, driven by their self-preservative instinct to the limits of human passion.

In vain Dr. Stern tried to stop them. His voice was drowned in the roar. Helplessly we remained pinned to the door.

We knew that the hospital had suffered a direct hit. We could smell the smoke, and we could see the flicker of fire through the blown-out windows. But how badly were we hit? What was the extent of the damage? Were there any victims? We could not tell yet. Crazed hundreds fought their way to the shelter, not permitting us to move or to take command of the situation.

"They'll kill one another. They'll trample one another to death," Dr. Stern kept saying, unable to do anything, but look on helplessly.

As the mob spilled down the staircase, many fell under the pressure. They were trampled underfoot. Screams of pain emanated from the stairwell while we waited powerlessly for this mad herd to thin out. There was a gunshot somewhere below us. Who used the gun? Why?

The smoke rolled now in thick, round, gray clouds. I began to cough. I, too, began to feel the need to run, to escape, to hide from this inferno. I ventured out. Immediately I was caught in the torrent and swept by it toward the stairs.

If I can only stay on my feet, I prayed. "Comrades, comrades," I shouted, "stop running. There is no more danger." But my thin voice was lost in the pandemonium.

At the staircase I briefly saw an even more horrible picture. The whole wide stairway all the way down was filled with a sea of uncontrollable men. The railings shook and threatened to break. Nothing could stop them now. The avalanche carried me down the stairs. I felt my body being lifted, pushed, squeezed and crushed. I had no power of my own.

Shurik! I thought suddenly. *Where is he?* A new fear seized me. My Shurik! He would have no chance were he caught in this insane onrush.

Somehow, the crowd carried me to the steel doors of the basement and inside. It was pitch-dark in the shelter. It was full of people and more of them piled in, but it was surprisingly quiet. The shouts and curses were absent, as if the darkness had a soothing effect on the turbulence within the men.

A trace of smoke wafted into the shelter, but, otherwise, the basement was apparently not damaged. I found myself pressed to the wall. Feeling my way along it, I crept to the center of the huge basement, knowing that there was a wall cabinet with flashlights and first aid kits. As I worked my way toward the cabinet, I kept talking to the soldiers I couldn't see, trying to sound calm and friendly. At last I reached the cabinet and was able to take out a flashlight.

I pointed the beam of the light toward my own face and shouted, "You are all safe here, comrades. Just stay where you are and don't push. Are there any nurses here?" From several corners came the replies of the nurses: "Natasha here." "Zoya." "Vera." "Lucya."

"Good. Stay here with the patients until I find out what's going on outside. Did anyone see Shurik?" I yelled over the din of the crowd.

"Here I am, at the back door." I heard his high voice.

"Are you all right?"

"Yes."

Thank God, I thought. "Stay where you are, Shurik, until you hear from me," I shouted. I began inching my way toward the steel door.

On the staircase there was a group of people, crowding around a prone figure, lying on the stone floor. I saw Dr. Stern kneeling beside it.

"What happened?" I asked.

"Commissar Churakov—they trampled him to death."

"My God. How horrible. How did it happen?"

"He was, apparently, trying to stop the panic. He shot his gun in the air, hoping to stop them," said Dr. Stern, getting up from his knees with effort. He held the commissar's gun. I looked down at the battered body of our handsome, kind commissar.

What chance did he have, this gallant, one-legged veteran, to stop an avalanche of panicked men? I thought as tears clouded my vision. The commissar's crutch lay beside him, snapped in two like a matchstick. His cane was nowhere to be seen.

"Any other casualties?" I asked Dr. Stern.

"Yes. Three more dead on the staircase and scores of newly hurt and wounded. And two wards totally demolished."

"And the patients in those wards?"

"All dead."

A chill shook my body. "Where do you want me to work?" I asked Dr. Stern.

"Stay with me. We'll work in the operating room, and Dr. Yakovlev and Zina will take over the reception room. But first, I must go and see for myself what other damage we have sustained. Where is Shurik?"

"He is in the shelter. He's OK."

"Thank God for that. How did he get there?" he asked.

"I don't know, but he is OK."

"Let's go, then." Dr. Stern began to climb the stairs. Mamma Lisa covered the dead commissar with a sheet.

"The fire is completely extinguished," reported the fire chief to Dr. Stern. "It was a minor fire, anyway. The civil defense workers have arrived and are helping my men to clear up the debris and search for survivors. Although I doubt that they will be able to find anyone. The bomb hit your west wing and sliced it right to the ground."

"Yes, I can see it myself," the doctor said wearily.

It was an awesome sight. From the top of the roof to the street level, the left wing of our four-story building was sliced, like a theater set. The thick steel beams, which once formed the skeleton of the building, had been snapped and twisted as if they had been nothing more than toy erector-set parts broken by a destructive child. A layer of fine, pink brick dust covered the street. Heaps of rubble lay in the street about the hospital. Shattered glass crushed noisily under our feet. The whole street sparkled with it, as if it were still covered with ice.

Three or four dozen men and *Komsomol* girls scurried around the ruins with shovels and crowbars. They were digging in the debris, searching for survivors. *Who could have survived a direct hit?* I thought. *If one were not killed outright, one would surely die under tons of falling bricks.*

The mound of dead bodies, dug from the rubble, grew rapidly.

"We'll need two trucks to remove them," the fire chief commented authoritatively. "How many men would you say you had in this section?"

Dr. Stern looked at me. "What was the morning census?" I couldn't remember it, but knowing that there were sixty beds in the west wing, it was a safe guess that all of them had been filled. It was our section for the seriously wounded.

Dr. Stern sighed deeply. "Well, comrade, I'll leave it all in your capable hands. I must go back to the living. We have many new wounded to treat, due to this terrible panic. So do what you must, and report to me."

"Don't worry, doctor, we'll put a temporary fence around here so no one will come poking about. We'll remove the dead and give you a receipt. I will write a report for the military headquarters and have you cosign it. You just go, and patch up the poor fellows up there."

We left. Indeed, there was nothing that we could do out here. Inside, there were dozens of men in need of our help.

"How did you ever get down to the shelter?" I asked Shurik several hours later when some semblance of order was restored.

"By the back stairs," he said. "The main staircase was so crowded that I knew we would never make it."

Crowded, I thought. *He calls it "crowded."* The sweet innocence of childhood. Then another thought occurred to me. "You said 'we.' Who do you mean by 'we'?"

"The patients and Uncle Kolya Polivanov."

"How did he get there?" I couldn't conceive of Polivanov, weak as he was, getting through the panic-stricken herd of men into the shelter three stories below.

"By the back stairs, I told you." Shurik was impatient with my slowness of comprehension. "I told the men to support Uncle Kolya and help him walk."

"How many of you were there?"

"I don't know." Shurik puckered his brow, thinking. "I believe, there were all the patients from wards five and six—and Uncle Kolya, of course."

Forty-one men in all, I thought. *My boy led forty-one men to safety, without a single injury to anyone of them.*

"How did you do it?" I asked.

"Well, when I heard someone yell 'Fire,' I was at the nurses' station in ward five. So I opened the door and saw all the men rushing down. I knew there were other stairs, in the back, leading straight to the basement. I peeked down the staircase and found no one using it."

"And then?"

"Then I told the wounded, 'Let's go down. I'll show you the way.' And they all went. Uncle Kolya was terribly weak. He couldn't even stand up. So I asked two soldiers to hold him up, and they did. When we came into the shelter, it was still empty. I opened the steel door. There was a noise and I knew that the crowd was almost there."

"The main door was locked?"

"No, it was just closed, but Uncle Kolya said, 'Go and open it, quickly, or they'll break it down.' So I did." Shurik sounded so nonchalant that I knew he was completely unaware of his heroism. Forty-one men. He brought forty-one men to safety.

"Were you scared?" I asked him.

"No. I know when a bomb hits the worst is over. Besides, it all happened so fast. I had no time to get scared. I was too busy."

He had no time to get scared, I thought with admiration. *In this phrase he expressed everything.* He was too busy working, performing his duty. He had no time to be scared.

"But what about the fire? Weren't you scared when you smelled smoke?" I asked, overwhelmed with the need to know.

"There is always a smell of smoke when a bomb hits. I just thought that someone yelled 'Fire,' out of mischief, like we did at school."

My God, this child has the coolest head among us all, I thought with pride.

"I was worried about Snezhinka," Shurik confessed. "She was in Dr. Stern's office, as usual, but I didn't know if they would remember to keep the door closed. She was probably scared to death by the commotion."

I laughed for the first time since our disaster. "Yes, she was scared, I'm sure, but not enough to forget to bark," I said, remembering her furious yelps. "Anyhow, dear, run along now, I must go to the staff meeting."

"And I must go and see Uncle Kolya," said my boy, with all the seriousness of an adult. "He was very weak when we brought him upstairs."

"You do that," I said, turning to go.

"And you check on Snezhinka," said Shurik. "I was able to see her only for a minute after the panic. She must feel very lonely."

"I'll pet her, don't worry, but most likely, she is curled up on Dr. Stern's lap, if I know our Snezhinka!"

Shurik laughed and ran up the stairs, trying to span two steps at a time.

"Our losses are great," began Dr. Stern, when all the senior officers assembled in his office. "But the greatest and the most senseless of all is the death of our commissar." There were tears in the colonel's eyes, and he made no effort to hide them.

"I don't blame anyone for what has happened today. No one could have foreseen the panic. No one could have prevented it. We all witnessed helplessly how our patients maimed and even killed one another in the grip of their turmoil. One of us tried to stop them. He paid with his life for this attempt." Dr. Stern fell silent for a moment, staring into his boarded-up window. "We have other casualties, too, due to the panic. You have the list, Mamma Lisa, please read it to us."

She placed her round, steel spectacles on her short nose and read from the daily journal: "Twenty broken arms. Three broken legs. One broken jaw. Seventy-five patients with wounds reopened. One nurse—Maya—broken toe. Sixty patients from the critical wards in the west wing dead. The only wards without any casualties are five and six. The patients were led to the shelter via the back stairs by Shurik."

"What?" cried Dr. Stern, suddenly standing up behind his desk. Snezhinka, who indeed was on his lap, fell down with a shrill yelp. "What do you mean—led by Shurik?"

Mamma Lisa shrugged her shoulders. "I don't know the details, but the men in five and six told me that Shurik led them down to the shelter in an orderly way and without casualties. Perhaps the lieutenant knows more about it?" She looked at me.

"Do you?" demanded Dr. Stern, sitting down again and slapping his knee for Snezhinka to jump back.

"Yes, I do," I said willingly. "It seems that Shurik was the only one who didn't lose his head and remembered that there was another set of stairs leading to the basement. So he calmly told the patients to follow him, which they did. Not only did he lead forty men out of wards five and six, but he even arranged for Polivanov to be helped down to the basement."

I saw smiles spread on the faces of the staff members.

"What a boy," exclaimed Dr. Stern finally. "If it were up to me, I would give him the highest medal for bravery."

That night, on the way home, I was able to see again the extent of the destruction to our hospital. The whole wing was gone. A tall, plywood fence surrounded the ruins and protruded to the center of the street. Obviously not all the wreckage behind it was yet removed. But the pile of dead bodies was gone as was the thick carpet of broken glass.

"It must have been a thousand-pounder," cried Shurik. "Look how it sliced the building. Like a knife. Only a thousand-pound bomb can do that." He sounded as if he were an authority on the tonnage of demolition bombs.

"Uncle Kolya says that the Fritzes are desperate. They couldn't starve us, so they are trying to destroy us from the air. But they'll never do it, will they?" He looked at me searchingly.

"No, they'll never do it. But let's not think of that. Let's think of something more pleasant. For instance, how would you like to go to the concert with me?"

"When is the concert?"

"Tomorrow eveninng."

"OK, I'll go with you. It's better than sitting alone, worrying about you when you're out," he said, sounding like an old, grouchy grandpa.

"Good!" I smiled. "Tomorrow you'll have your first exposure to the Leningrad Philharmonic Orchestra or, rather, to the remnants of it, from all that I hear."

It was indeed true, that what used to be one of the best Russian symphony orchestras was no more. Death, starvation and active duty in the armed forces robbed the Philharmonic Orchestra of 95 percent of its artists. Before the war we had three major orchestras in the city, in addition to the philharmonic. Now, among all four of them, there were only twenty musicians left. Obviously, nothing much could have been done with only twenty musicians. The city government decided to hold auditions for the vacancies in the reactivated Philharmonic Orchestra. Sixty-four musicians replied. Thus, a new orchestra was born. Immediately they began their rehearsals. Some of the musicians were so weak that they had to be helped to their seats on the stage. They were enrolled in *stazionari* for extra nutrition. Many of them were billeted in dormitories and put under doctors' care for they were suffering from varying degrees of dystrophy, the dread disease of our siege. Now, most of it was over. Tomorrow they were to perform their first concert.

I felt a little uncertain when, next day, I asked Dr. Stern for a moment of his time to discuss something personal.

"Would it be too frivolous of me to attend a concert at a time of such tragedy at our hospital? I don't want to be considered callous, and yet, I would like very much to go," I said.

"Of course you must go, my dear. There is nothing more to be done but carry on in our routine way. Take the evening off and enjoy yourself. You need a little relaxation. I wish I could go, too. Maybe next time. Too much paper work piled up for me."

"Thank you for your consideration. I'll tell you all about the concert. Or, better yet, Shurik will tell you."

The, concert was to take place in the Pushkin Drama Theater. The Philharmonic Hall, hit by an artillery shell, had not yet been restored to its prewar splendor. The Pushkin Theater was used by the actors of a musical comedy group throughout the blockade. They continued to give performances for the troops even during the worst weeks of the siege.

Shurik and I approached the theater from the less glamorous side, where the artists' entrances were. The Pushkin Drama Theater was the first place that I worked as an extra while still a student at the Leningrad Institute of Theater Arts.

"Here is the ballet school." I pointed to a long building with classical columns on the right side of the street. "When I was your age, I dreamt of becoming a ballerina. If I hadn't been already enrolled at the Academic Capella school for musically gifted children, I would probably have been a student at the ballet school."

"It's not for me. I'll be a doctor," he said resolutely. "Or maybe a forest conservationist."

"A forest conservationist! Where did you get that new ambition?"

"From Uncle Kolya. He'll be a forest conservationist when he gets home. He used to be a lumberjack but now, because he'll be limping, he won't be able to cut trees anymore. So he'll plant trees instead. That's what he told me."

"It's very interesting. Where is he from?"

"Somewhere on the Kama River. He says he lived in the woods all his life. He doesn't like big cities."

We entered the lobby and presented our tickets to an usher.

Oh, to be an actress again, I thought longingly.

"You wish you were an actress again, don't you?" said Shurik, with an uncanny insight into my thoughts. I squeezed his hand tightly and nodded. We watched the theater fill with a motley crowd, dressed in heavy winter clothing. There were hundreds of military men and women. Some of them arrived in formations and went to their seats still carrying their automatic rifles.

The stage was open. The heavy crimson curtain was parted, and we could see the plain chairs and music stands arranged in the traditional manner of symphonic concerts. There was a conductor's podium with narrow railing, covered with balding red velvet.

The musicians began to enter the stage and the cacophony of tuning filled the air. I watched the musicians. They were all, without exception, pale and emaciated. A few women were among them, particularly in the string section. All were dressed in formal white tie and tails, or black evening gowns, but shod in a wide variety of footwear. Some wore patent-leather formal shoes, while the others wore whatever they had, including a few *valenki.* One of the violinists even wore homemade carpet slippers. Obviously his feet were still swollen from scurvy—a dreaded disease caused by vitamin deficiency. Most of them wore mittens to keep their fingers warm up to the last minute. Some kept their mittens on even during the tuning of instruments. The icy cold of the theater obviously deprived them of the normal agility of their fingers.

The concertmaster stood up and gave the signal for a clarinetist to sound an "A." The whole orchestra repeated the note and its variations, then hushed. The conductor entered the stage. He was greeted with a burst of applause. Somehow, we all felt that we were witnessing a significant historic moment: the first concert after the devastating winter of hunger and death. Despite everything, we were living. We were about to partake of something beautiful, immortal. We were about to hear music.

It was a short program, consisting of four or five numbers of Russian classical music. It ended with the rousing overture to Glinka's *Ruslan and Ludmila*. The members of the orchestra stood up to acknowledge the applause of the enthusiastic audience.

"Is it already over?" Shurik asked disappointedly.

"Yes, I'm afraid it is. But don't worry, there will be other concerts. After all, this was the very first one, and as you can see, the musicians are tired."

"I will go to the concerts again and again, and I'll learn how to conduct," Shurik chatted excitedly.

"What? You want to be an orchestra conductor now? What happened to your being a doctor or a forest conservationist?"

"I could be all three," Shurik declared, undaunted. "I can conserve forests in the summer and conduct orchestras in the winter."

"And when are you going to take care of the sick?" He looked perplexed for a moment but then brightened up as a new idea occurred to him.

"In the spring and in the autumn. That's when most people catch cold and need a doctor," he cried triumphantly.

"Well, you certainly have your future well planned," I said, laughing.

Shurik had a dreamy expression. I was sure he was seeing himself on the podium with a thin, ivory baton in his hand, a full symphony orchestra at his feet, ready to follow his every move, responding with majestic sounds. I had to smile into my army coat collar. I almost saw it myself.

13

The tempo of life was accelerating. On April fifteenth we heard once again the gay clanking of streetcars. Several strategic lines had been repaired, the tracks were freed from stranded cars and traffic was resumed. Two power stations were put back in operation which began transmitting electricity to our homes for a few hours a day. Water pipes, too, were under mass repair. Hundreds of young *Komsomol* girls were given quick courses in plumbing, and one could see them scurrying around the city with acetylene torches in their hands, thawing out the water mains and sewer pipes. "In a few weeks we will have running water again," the survivors of the horrible winter promised one another with dreamy expressions.

Food rations continued to improve. Not only did we have enough bread now, but we were getting real meat, butter and sugar, in addition to macaroni, flour and potatoes. But vegetables and fruits were still unavailable. As a result, we all suffered from deficiency of vitamin C.

Then it was announced on the radio that there was plenty of vitamin C in pine needles. The city government once again called on all able-bodied women and children for help. They were to go to the woods to gather pine branches. The pine needles were to be processed to produce a strong extract of vitamin C for distribution.

The Road of Life ceased its existence during the last week of April. The ice became too treacherous to permit the convoys to cross the lake. For several days horse-driven sledges were allowed to traverse Ladoga, but they carried only half loads. During the day the ice was covered with a thin layer of melting water, and the drivers had to wear galoshes over their *valenki*. At night the water froze again, making the road into one slippery ice field, where horses and men broke their legs and sledges crashed. With every passing hour, the supply route became more dangerous until finally, on April twenty-fourth, all traffic across the lake was halted.

Now we awaited the opening of navigation across Ladoga. As soon as the ice would flow into the Baltic, sometime in the middle of May, we would have many barges, towed by sturdy tugboats, plying the waters of the lake. They would quadruple the flow of supplies into our still encircled city.

Meanwhile, the Germans introduced something new into their attacks on Leningrad. For the first time we became the targets of their dive bombers. Maybe at the front it was nothing new, but to us, in the city, this method became full of morbid fascination. People stood in every doorway, watching enemy planes go into a dive, as if it were not a screeching, whistling death coming at them, but rather, some daredevil demonstration of a new technique. Indeed, it looked frightening only when one was within the immediate zone of the enemy attack. Otherwise, one had the detached feeling of being an observer at an air show. For the planes no longer came in huge waves. The dive bombers came in threes and fives and occasionally in sixes or sevens. Gone were the days when wave after wave of Nazi planes dropped their deadly load on our city, the raid lasting for hours. The dive bombers did their job quickly, rarely returning for a second or third run over the target. They were gone from the skies as fast as they appeared.

It was indeed fascinating to watch the dive bombers. One after another they would break away from the formation and, screeching louder and louder, hurl themselves down through the air, like birds of prey on their unsuspecting victim below. Their most favored target was a string of naval ships which wintered in the city along the embankment. But the ships were well-prepared for them. They met them with all the fire power they had, including machine guns. Not one ship was sunk, although there were several minor hits. Surprisingly, too, there was very little damage to the beautiful palaces, including the famous museum, the Hermitage. The buildings lined the Neva's embankments and thus were in the direct target zone of the planes. I often shuddered at the thought of the possibility of losing our Hermitage. It was so vulnerable there, next to the stranded ships.

"*Ledokhód!* The ice has moved," shouted Shurik. "The radio just announced that the ice has moved. I have never seen *ledokhód!* May I go?" It was still early in the morning and, if we hurried, I thought we might make it to the river before going to the hospital.

"All right, hurry up then," I said. "We'll have a bite to eat at work."

We were the sole occupants of my communal apartment now. All the tenants of this five-room flat were dead. It felt strange to live alone in what once was a bustling hive, filled with people. Our footsteps echoed loudly as we crossed the large kitchen, empty and cold. Only a few months ago five different kerosene stoves used to hum in unison, filling the kitchen with warmth and delicious smells of cooking. The housewives chatted amicably with one another. Now, all were gone. Snezhinka's barks sounded loud and shrill in the empty apartment. No one was there to complain.

We locked all the doors thoroughly. It was even more dangerous now to live alone. Gangs were known to break into empty apartments and strip them of everything, including heavy furniture. It was snowing again. The snow, heavy with moisture, fell on our faces in thick, wet flakes. The air smelled of the south wind indicating that soon the snow would turn into spring rain. On the Palace Bridge there were already many people. They lined up along the sculptured railings of the bridge, all of them looking down.

We found a place and leaned on the railing. Below us, in a corridor of swiftly moving, steel-gray water, floated various-sized chunks of dirty, porous ice. From time to time one could see how this corridor would widen, as a huge floe would break away and drift toward the sea, away from the solid mass of ice which still bound the river.

It was a fascinating annual spectacle of nature, which the Leningraders never failed to watch. Even now, dozens of citizens lined up along the railings of the bridge, witnessing the spring thaw of river ice called the *ledokhód*. The watchers ignored the danger from enemy shells which continued to fall on the city.

"Let's go, Shurik. It's too wet and raw here. We'll catch colds," I said, tugging at his sleeve. But Shurik was fascinated with the swift movement of the ice floes.

"There will be another *ledokhód* in a week or two. The one from Ladoga. You can come again and watch. Maybe the weather will be better."

A streetcar was approaching, and we ran to catch it. We were not allowed inside because of Snezhinka, but it was still better to ride on the open platform than to trek in the wet snowstorm. Utterly soaked by now, we finally arrived at the hospital.

"Lieutenant, the new commissar wants to talk to you," said a young aide, meeting me at the entrance.

"I'll be right over." I changed into my hospital uniform and hurried to the commissar's office. He was assigned to us only three days before, but the morale of the patients and the staff, shattered by the tragedy of the recent bombing, was already improving.

He initiated the publishing of our own newspaper, *Na strázhe ródiny,* On Guard for the Motherland, which our recuperating patients would print by hand weekly. Shurik instantly became his Man Friday, running errands for him and drawing pictures for the paper. The commissar was a Georgian, with the long and difficult name of Gogishvili.

"Just call me Gogo," he told us with a dazzling smile. "No one can pronounce my name."

I liked Captain Gogo. He looked like a typical Georgian—of medium height, with a thin, almost girlish waistline which he kept tightly belted with a silver-encrusted belt. He wore a black *cherkésska,* the Georgian national dress, and to his ornate belt a real dagger was attached. He looked so dashing, so unreal among us in our drab olive-green uniforms. It made me smile, just to look at him in his colorful costume and shaggy-furred *papákha,* a tall hat. His eyes were coal-black and sparkling; his teeth, the whitest I had ever seen.

He spoke Russian with a strong Georgian accent, which always sounded hilarious to Russian ears. He looked almost theatrical in our midst, and yet, were he among his own people in Georgia, he would have been lost in the crowd. Georgians were all very picturesque people.

"You wanted to see me, Comrade Gogo?" I asked.

"Yes, please come in and close the door," he said, looking up at me from a sheet of paper he was reading. "I have here a petition from our patients concerning Shurik. I want to know what you think of it." He handed me a letter written in pencil.

The patients were requesting the headquarters of the Leningrad Front to award a medal to Shurik in recognition of his deed of bravery during the bombing of our hospital. There were only ten signatures on the letter, but the petitioners wrote that they were the elected representatives of the entire patient group.

"Do you think the staff will go along with signing the petition?"

"I'm sure of it. Everyone here adores Shurik," I exclaimed happily.

"All right, then," he said, standing up. "We'll pass this petition around until we collect several hundred signatures: it will look very impressive that way. Then Dr. Stern and I will write the official request for the decoration, describing in detail the circumstances and Shurik's participation in the events of April the fourth."

"Could we keep it secret?" I asked. "I mean, it would be terrible to raise Shurik's expectations. What if headquarters would deny our request?"

"Yes, we will keep it secret," he said. "But I think we won't be denied. Think of the propaganda value. A child, a mere ten-year-old, saves dozens of lives."

"It will be wonderful if they give him a medal," I said hopefully.

"Yes, and I think we have a pretty good chance of getting it for him. By the way, who are his parents and where are they? He is not your brother, is he?"

"No, no. Unfortunately, he is not my brother. His parents are both dead. His mother was killed during the bombing last November. His father was a gunner in a tank battalion and was killed in December. The boy is alone—except for his friends here."

"Too bad. But this fact will also help us in getting his medal. It will soften the toughest hearts at headquarters."

"You are too cynical."

"No, just realistic," he said.

The signatures of the entire contingent of patients and staff members were gathered in two nights. Dr. Stern added his own letter of recommendation, describing also Shurik's daily work with the patients. The request was dispatched to headquarters by a special messenger.

Meanwhile, the first of May, the traditional national holiday had arrived. During peacetime we always had parades on the Palace Square. Celebrations occurred throughout the city. The fleet, which always came into the Neva for the holidays, would put on a dazzling display of fireworks. But that was before the war.

On this May Day in 1942 we had no holiday. The fleet was on the river as usual, but not to celebrate but rather to hide from the enemy. And yet, there was a holidaylike mood in the air. Maybe it was because there were proclamations pasted on the walls of buildings announcing a special holiday ration of sweets and other items of food. Maybe it was because the weather finally turned warm and sunny, bringing hope to our hearts.

Shurik and I took Snezhinka for a short walk in the park near Kazan Cathedral. Every square inch of ground, which once was covered with flowers, was now planted with vegetables. The city government allocated all the parks, gardens and empty lots for growing vegetables by the Leningraders. The seeds were flown in from the mainland. Our people, barely able to move after the long winter of starvation, began to dig thousands of small plots by hand, to plant cabbages and potatoes. Although it was an early spring, they were thinking ahead of another winter of blockade.

No one wanted to talk about it openly, but many thought of it constantly, while they dug in the earth in public parks and planted the seeds. We walked along the paths, watching the frail people working or sunning themselves in the park.

So few of us are left, I thought as I glanced around me. Thousands of citizens were already evacuated from Leningrad, and many more would be sent away over Ladoga during the navigable months of summer and early fall. Only a token number would remain to endure the blockade which would last for nearly two more winters. But luckily, no one knew about it on that sunny first day of May.

"Do you think I could snap a branch of lilac for Uncle Kolya?" Shurik asked me, pulling the fragrant branch to his nose. No one was in sight.

"Let me do it," I said, swiftly breaking off a small branch. Looking about us guiltily, we slipped out of the park, hoping that no one had seen us.

Shurik brought the lilac branch to Polivanov and placed it on the table in a medicine bottle. Polivanov smiled broadly. He was progressing quickly now. Dr. Stern was going to move him into R section, since he no longer needed special care.

"Where did you get it?" he demanded.

"We stole it," cried Shurik, enjoying his participation in a bit of lawlessness.

"Lilacs . . . *sierén.* We have bunches of them growing around our houses in Sierénevka. Even our village is named after them." He fell silent, thinking of his home village.

"Where is Sierénevka?" I asked.

"On the Kama. It is the most beautiful section of the whole country up there," he said with pride.

"Tell us about your country, Uncle Kolya," begged Shurik. "Kyra never heard your stories."

"Well, someday, after the war, you must come and visit with us in Sierénevka. You'll like it there. And you, young man, you will go wild with joy in our woods."

"Are there thick woods, like taigá?" I asked.

"Oh, yes, we have hundreds of miles of thick woods on both sides of the river. There are villages here and there and planted fields, too, but mainly, it is one continuous forest. Of course, near Perm and Krasnokamsk, there are a lot of villages," he said, as if apologizing for bragging about the forest. "But I don't like it near the cities."

"I told you, didn't I?" cried Shurik. "Uncle Kolya only likes the woods or the river."

"Tell me, isn't it true that Kama is considered a European river, rather than an Asiatic one, since it is on the western side of the Ural Mountains?"

"Yes, people say so. But we Uralians, we think of ourselves as Asiatics. Russians—but Asiatics."

Shurik was bored with the development of our discussion.

"Tell us about the river," he begged.

"I think that the Kama is the most beautiful river in the whole Soviet Union," he began. "Before the war, I used to work *na plotákh,* on rafts, floating timber along the river. Oh, what a glorious, free life it was!" he sighed. "We used to go into the forest in the winter and cut the thick, tall trees. Then, with the first warm weather, we would return to the woods and tie those huge trunks together with heavy chains and spikes, making rafts. Then, a tugboat would come chugging along and we would string the rafts one after another in a long train. We would build small cabins on the rafts, where we would live for several weeks, floating along the river. Beautiful!" he said dreamily.

"How did your wife like it when you were away from home for such long periods?" I asked.

"I took her with me whenever possible. She cooked for the crew. She enjoyed it—going *na plotákh*. My kids loved it too! We took our chickens with us, and a goat and our dogs. My little daughter even took her kitten along."

"All on the raft?"

"All on the raft! We had fresh eggs and goat's milk, and plenty of berries and mushrooms from the woods. We had a little tin stove and, of course, the campfire. We fished and fried our catch over the open fire. Great life."

"Campfire on the raft? Weren't you afraid to burn your raft?"

"No. We had an iron plate over which we built a little brick pit. Very simple."

"And if it rained?" Shurik demanded.

"If it rained, we stayed right in the cabin, drank vodka, and sang songs!"

"I wish I could go on such a raft someday," Shurik said, entranced.

"Come and visit me, and you'll go, I promise you," said Polivanov. "Although I myself will never be a logger again. I'll be a cripple instead," he added bitterly.

"Don't talk like that, Uncle Kolya," Shurik interrupted. "You'll be planting trees now. Remember? You told me."

Polivanov laughed, still bitterly. "Yes, I'll plant little saplings now instead of felling huge giants. Quite a change for a strong man," he said, closing his eyes wearily.

"Come, Shurik, let's go," I said quietly. "Comrade Polivanov must be tired." We left his room.

I could see that his future bothered him. It must be hard for a powerful man to reconcile himself to a limited life. I could almost see in my mind's eye this giant of a man, his muscles rippling, glistening with perspiration, on top of a long raft, floating down the calm waters of the wide Kama.

"He is just like my father," Shurik was saying. "He even looks like him. Big. With strong hands. Do you think he is dead?"

I was taken completely by surprise. To stall for time to gather my wits, I mumbled, "Who do you mean?"

Shurik looked at me impatiently. "My father, of course. Do you think he is dead? I have had no word from him since last November, when my mother was still alive." He spoke seriously and unemotionally. Now was the time to tell him the truth. The truth, which both Dr. Stern and I were unable to tell him all these weeks. I plunged into it.

"Yes, Shurik, your father was killed in action. Dr. Stern has a letter from your father's commander about it," I said carefully.

"I just knew it," Shurik said quietly.

I looked at his serious, lovely face, his sad, unchildlike eyes, and I began to cry. He put his arms around my waist and looked up at me.

"Don't cry," he said. "Everyone in Leningrad has lost someone. Sometimes I think that when the war is over, there won't be a single person who hasn't lost someone. But don't cry, please, or I'll start crying, too. I just knew that father was killed," repeated Shurik, shaking his head. "You see, I thought at first that maybe his letters were lost, since the house where we used to live didn't exist anymore. Then, I thought a bit about it, and I said to myself—*no, if Papa didn't hear anything from us he would have come to the city, even for a few hours, to find out whether we were still alive.* After all, the frontline is so near the city." He paused and looked straight into my face.

"Then I knew that he must have been killed. I didn't tell it to you, because I knew it would have upset you."

My dearest boy, I thought tenderly, *you were protecting me.*

I held him closely and swore to myself that I would never part from him.

"You won't send me away, will you?" I heard him say. "Now, that I'm a real orphan, you won't let them take me away?"

"No, my darling, I'll do everything to keep you with me forever." I stroked his bristly head. "I promise."

Commissar Gogo was the last one to arrive at Dr. Stern's office, although it was he who asked for a special meeting of the staff. He wore a secretive look, and he had about him an aura of pleasant expectation.

"Comrades, I have just received a directive from the front headquarters that Shurik is going to be awarded a medal—*Za Boyevóe Otlíchieye*—for bravery," he announced proudly.

"Great," exclaimed Dr. Stern with a broad smile.

"Now, comrades, we must make the most of this marvelous propaganda opportunity," continued the commissar earnestly. "I know some of you are ready to run and tell the good news to Shurik." He looked at me and winked. "But I want to keep it secret until the actual day of presentation. We'll have a real celebration. We'll have reporters from the front-line papers, and headquarters will send their own representative to award the medal to our young hero."

Dr. Stern had an indulgent expression. He listened to the commissar as if the latter were a young, enthusiastic student of his, making plans for a graduation party.

"We'll be famous—if we take advantage of this opportunity," Gogo continued. "Our hospital will be written about in papers. Maybe even in *Pravda*. And, who knows, maybe even abroad. The presentation of the medal will be held a week from today, on May twenty-second. If no one objects, I'll take it upon myself to prepare for this occasion. I know exactly what must be done."

No one objected.

The meeting was adjourned. We all pledged our fullest co-operation, leaving the details in the able hands of Commissar Gogishvili.

The night before Shurik's day of triumph, Dr. Stern allowed me to leave the hospital early. He wanted to have Shurik out of the way so that Commissar Gogo and his helpers could decorate the large ward where the presentation was to take place.

"Let's go for a walk," I suggested to Shurik. "The evening is so balmy. It feels like summer."

"Can we go and see the ships?"

I hesitated. The ships were constantly a target of enemy at-tacks. One went in that vicinity only when absolutely necessary.

"Please," begged Shurik. "I haven't seen the submarines. They were so frozen in the river that I could hardly distinguish them from the piled-up ice. Please?"

"Oh, all right! Only for a short time . . . You know how dangerous it is at the river during an air raid."

Snezhinka danced at our side, instinctively knowing that we were going for a walk. We went along Nevsky Prospect, toward the tall spire of the Admiralty. The submarine anchorage was along the Admiralty quay, in front of the monument to Peter the Great. We traversed the park with its statuary of mythological gods and goddesses representing the sea. We breathed deeply the fragrant scent of linden trees just coming into bloom.

Along the paths, where grass once grew, thick and abundant, there were even rows of tiny vegetable plots. People's private kitchen gardens—*ogorodi*. The plantings were just sprouting, and one could see the lines of bright green protruding through the dark soil of the park. On the benches along the paths sat motionless figures of watchmen. People didn't trust one another, and they stayed in the park until curfew, guarding their seedlings from one another.

We left the park and entered the square. Here stood the majestic statue of Peter the Great, erected in his memory by Catherine the Great. However, one could not see the statue now. It was hidden behind a wall of sandbags which were covered with several layers of thick boards. Only a direct hit could have destroyed it. Almost all the city monuments were protected in this way. Some of them, however, were removed from their pedestals and buried underground until better days.

"Do you know the story of the bronze horseman?" I asked Shurik.

"No. Tell me the story. I just love stories," he cried, his eyes lighting up with excitement.

"Well, unfortunately, we can't see the statue now, but when the war's over and the boards and sandbags are removed, you'll see then that only the horse's forelegs are shod.

"The story is that when Catherine the Great had this statue completed, she arrived at this square with her entourage for the unveiling. There were hundreds of people here who wanted to see the empress even more than the new sculpture. I'm sure it was all very ceremonious, with the mounted palace guards, flags and standards flying, ladies elegantly clad, and the empress herself in an elaborate powdered wig, riding in the royal golden carriage drawn by six white horses.

"After the canvas was removed from the statue, everyone expressed great admiration for it, a truly magnificent work of art. As you probably remember, Peter is depicted here in a Roman emperor's robes, a laurel wreath on his brow, astride a rearing steed, his arm raised, pointing forward. A serpent is coiled at the horse's hind legs, representing the evil forces which stood in the path of Peter's desire to open 'a window to Europe.' "

"What do you mean? A window to Europe?"

"That was Peter's way of saying that Russia must look to

Europe for new ideas. You see, he was the first Russian tsar who saw how backward and poor Russia was. So, he built a new city—St. Petersburg, which we now call Leningrad. He built it on the Baltic Sea, so that we would have a direct connection with Europe."

"Oh, now I see. He sort of opened the window, to let the fresh air in. Fresh air means new ideas?"

"Right. But anyhow, while Catherine received congratulations for this monument, she suddenly noticed a little old peasant in the crowd, who just shook his head as if he didn't like the sculpture.

" 'Bring that man to me!' she commanded her handsome footman.

"The old peasant was seized and unceremoniously dragged before the empress.

" 'Don't you like our statue?' she demanded.

" 'Oh, yes, it's beautiful, Your Majesty, but it's not right.'

" 'Why is it not right?'

" 'Because our great Tsar Peter could not go far on this horse.'

" 'Why not?'

" 'Have you ever seen an unshod horse go far? No. Never. The horse would start limping.'

"The empress thought for a moment and then she burst out laughing. Her ladies in waiting, her ministers, her guards, footmen, they all laughed, too, although they knew not why.

" 'Give the good man ten rubles in gold and shoe the horse. He is right. We can't let the Great Peter's horse go limping!'

"Unfortunately, the hind legs of the horse were securely attached to the granite pedestal. Thus, only the two forelegs, those which are rearing into the air, were shod with two especially-made horseshoes. So this is the story!"

"Do you think it's a true story?" asked Shurik eagerly.

"I don't know. I wasn't there."

We walked around the boarded monument, seeing in our imagination the great empress and the old peasant. A group of starlings dashed over our heads with shrill cries and settled for the night under the cornices of the stately old Senate building. We came to the steps leading to the water where three submarines gently rocked, one next to the other.

A young armed sailor stood guard at the steps.

"No farther," he warned, pointing his bayoneted rifle at us.

"Oh, all right," said Shurik. "I saw submarines when they were here before the war. But I was little. I didn't appreciate it then."

We crossed the street back to the buildings. I was sure that other ships were similarly guarded, and it was no use trying to go closer to them.

We walked farther along the embankment until we reached the Hermitage. An air raid siren sounded from the roof of the Winter Palace. We had to take refuge in the Hermitage bomb shelter, for we were caught in the most dangerous section of the city—the embankment.

The only people in the shelter were the workers of the Hermitage who lived on the premises. They all knew one another, and they looked at us with friendly curiosity. Not often were they exposed to a little boy with a fluffy dog in their intellectual midst.

I watched with interest this gathering of emaciated elderly men wearing the traditional skullcaps of the Academies of Sciences and Art. There were a few women, too, thin and pale. I heard that only in February were the intellectuals in the Hermitage given extra rations above the norm. No wonder they still looked half dead compared to the factory workers and military personnel who benefited from additional food much earlier.

"Who are you?" a bushy-bearded old man asked me. I introduced myself.

"And I'm Professor Luchinsky," he said, extending his birdlike hand.

"I know. I met you before the war when Professor Amosov and I gave a concert of Renaissance music and Boccaccio readings at the Hermitage Theater."

"Oh, yes. I remember. It was a charming evening. But what are you doing in the army? You should work in your own profession—theater!" He sounded almost angry. "We have millions of soldiers to fight in the war. People like you would be much more useful for the war effort working in their own métier. You should be performing for the troops."

"Yes, Professor Luchinsky, I agree, but——"

"There can be no argument about it. Let me introduce you to our distinguished director, Academic Orbeli." The professor grabbed my arm and pulled me toward a short man with a graying beard, wearing the inevitable academic cap, like a surgeon's, but rather made of dull black silk.

"So, this is the famous Academic Orbeli." I was overwhelmed with respect and awe at being in the presence of such elevated academic rank, the highest possible.

Academic Orbeli shook my hand. "And who is this?" he asked, looking at Shurik.

"This is my ward, Shurik Nikanorov." Orbeli patted Shurik on the head and then took a piece of candy, wrapped in a colorful foil paper, out of his pocket.

"I'm sure you like candy," he said, giving it to Shurik.

"Thank you, I do." Snezhinka almost snatched the candy from his hand, and Orbeli smacked her on the nose.

"That's the first dog I've seen in many months," he said to Luchinsky.

"Everybody says that," Shurik declared proudly. "We should make a statue of Snezhinka. The only dog in Leningrad." Everyone laughed as Orbeli patted Shurik's head once more.

Outside the antiaircraft guns of our ships were firing rapidly at the Nazi planes over the Neva. We could hear the deep thuds of explosions, but the vaulted subterranean shelters of the Hermitage were safe. I could see that the museum personnel had lived and worked in the shelters for months. There were cots everywhere, and tables, covered with books, papers, typewriters and other paraphernalia of art scholars. The interconnected cavernous shelters were like a small underground city, where many people carried on the work begun before the war.

"Were you able to evacuate most of the treasures from the Hermitage?" I asked Academic Orbeli. "I remember walking along the quay early in August with my mother and seeing trucks being loaded with paintings and sculptures. It was then that we felt for the first time how dangerous our situation at the front was becoming."

"Yes," he said, "we were able to evacuate several trainloads of treasures, but we still had to store quite a lot right here, in our own vaults. You can see some of the crates for yourself. They are actually all around here." Indeed, I could see dozens of packing crates of all sizes around the shelter. *So these are the boxes with priceless objects,* I thought with a feeling of reverence, for like most Russians I was brought up with deep respect and admiration for objects of art.

An all-clear signal sounded over the radio. With regret, I bade good-by to our hosts at the Hermitage bomb shelter.

"Remember what I told you about your role in the war," said Professor Luchinsky, shaking my hand. "I'll write to the Committee on Art Affairs requesting your reassignment."

14

Next morning we were met by Dr. Stern, who was walking back and forth in front of the hospital.

"I'm exercising," he explained to us jovially. "Care to walk with me?" he asked Shurik.

"Gladly." They joined hands and disappeared around the bombed section of the hospital. Snezhinka, who followed me inside, noticed the absence of her young master and dashed after him, barking loudly.

Commissar Gogo was waiting for me in the reception room.

"Everything is ready. Just keep Shurik out of the big ward until the representative from headquarters arrives. Where is he, by the way?" he asked in sudden alarm.

"He is walking around the block with Dr. Stern."

"Good. The photographers from the front-line papers are here already." He ran to the front door to greet a portly man in a major's uniform just emerging from a car.

"I'm Commissar Kozhin," I heard the man introduce himself.

I went to the dressing room to change. I heard the hum of many voices as I dressed. The wounded, those who could walk, were gathering in the big ward, once the school gymnasium, to witness the ceremony. As I entered the ward I found that every bit of space was filled with patients. There must have been at least 250 soldiers and personnel there.

Above the heads of the spectators stretched a long banner. Printed on it, in huge black letters, was written: LONG LIVE SHURIK, THE YOUNGEST HERO OF LENINGRAD. At the far end of the ward, in front of the boarded windows, stood a table, covered with red cloth. Behind it sat Commissar Kozhin— next to two empty chairs, for Dr. Stern and Shurik, undoubtedly. Near the table there were several men with cameras—photographers from army papers.

I made my way to the beds in the front row, where I noticed the friendly face of Polivanov. He was brought in on a portable bed. I perched on the corner of it. Commissar Gogo stood up and raised his hand. The noise of talk among the people subsided.

"Comrades——" he began, but was interrupted by the excited cry of Natasha, our lookout at the door. "They are coming. They are already on the stairs."

"Don't forget, all together, the National Anthem," the commissar shouted as the door opened.

Dr. Stern and Shurik, holding Snezhinka in his arms, entered the ward. Simultaneously the air was filled with the sounds of the National Anthem, played by the patients on their pocket combs covered with cigarette paper. I noticed that every soldier who could hold a comb had one and blew into it with gusto, producing the off-key rendition of the familiar melody. The cacophony was indescribable. I saw Zina take her own comb out of her hair and join the chorus. Her hair, left without anchor, fell to her shoulders like a cascade of ripe wheat.

Dr. Stern took bewildered Shurik by the hand and led him toward the table. Our commissar sprang to attention, and I saw Shurik's eyes widen in disbelief when he realized that the com-

missar was saluting him, rather than Dr. Stern. Snezhinka was
at first frightened by the noise, but seeing that it didn't come any
closer to her, joined in, adding her own shrill yaps to the general
bedlam. I saw Dr. Stern pointing out the slogan to Shurik. I
observed a slow blush of pleasure and embarrassment spread over
Shurik's face when he realized that he was, indeed, the center of
attention for this occasion.

Finally Commissar Gogo raised his hand again as the last
stanza came to an end.

"Comrades," Commissar Gogo began, "allow me to introduce
to you the comrade from the headquarters of the Leningrad
Front, Major Kozhin."

Commissar Kozhin stood up behind the table and, looking
sternly at Shurik, gestured to him to stand also. Shurik paled.
He slowly rose to his feet, still with Snezhinka in his arms.

"Shurik Nikanorov," the visiting commissar said in a sonorous
official-sounding voice, "in the name of the commander of the
Leningrad Front, I'm authorized to present you with a medal,
Za Boyevóye Otlíchiye. Come closer."

Shurik stepped closer to him, moving as if he had wooden legs.
I felt Polivanov stir. I glanced at him. His eyes were full of tears,
focused on Shurik.

Commissar Kozhin opened a small red box and took out a
shiny round medal on a colorful triangular ribbon. He pinned
the medal to Shurik's old sweater, above his heart. The "orchestra" burst out into a second rendition of the same anthem.
Obviously nothing else had been rehearsed for the occasion.
Those who could move rushed to Shurik to offer congratulations.

"Comrades, comrades, let the photographers take the pictures," I heard Commissar Gogo pleading. Discipline was restored at once, and the photographers began to snap their
pictures, making Commissar Kozhin repeat the medal-pinning
ceremony again and again.

Finally Dr. Stern stood up and said, "Comrades, we must disperse. Much as I would like to continue our pleasant gathering, we must disperse so that the tragedy which led to Shurik's decoration will never be repeated."

"The extraordinary meeting of our military hospital is adjourned," announced Commissar Gogo. Immediately nurses and aides began to carry the stretchers out as the walking patients followed. Soon the ward took on its usual look, except for the long banner which continued to sway gently over the beds, reminding the wounded of our little hero.

The hero, himself, was invited to Dr. Stern's office where a special breakfast awaited him. Only the two commissars, Dr. Stern, Shurik and I were to partake of this meal, but the whole population of the hospital was issued an extra ration of chocolate in honor of "Shurik's Day."

There wasn't much on our table at this special breakfast. Just the usual items from our rations—bread, sugar, hot porridge and tea. But Fyodor, our cook, managed to bake a small cake, with Shurik's name on it written in sugar.

"I can't get over it," Shurik kept repeating, cocking his head sideways, in order to see his medal. "Me, Shurik—a hero."

"You fully deserve the medal," declared Commissar Kozhin.

"Here is your certificate for the medal. Take care of it. Someday you'll show it to your grandchildren," he continued, giving Shurik a printed certificate with a reproduction of the medal on it. "Keep up the good work." He pinched Shurik's cheek and shook hands with us. He was in a hurry. He had to present more medals at the civil defense stations on the other side of the city. Commissar Gogo saw him off to his car.

We heard Kozhin's car sneeze and cough and, finally, with a noise like a firecracker exploding, tear out from the curb to its next destination.

"OK, Shurik, now that you are a famous person, what are

your feelings about it all?" asked Dr. Stern when we were left alone in his office.

"Feelings? I don't know. I guess I'm a little embarrassed."

"Embarrassed? But why?"

"Well—because I'm not a hero. I didn't kill any Nazis. I didn't shoot down any planes. So how can I be a hero?" He was sincere in his bewilderment.

"Let me tell you, Shurik. Come here." Dr. Stern stood Shurik between his knees and looked in his face with seriousness. "What you did that day, that is, bringing forty-one men to safety, was far more important than killing a Nazi. Without your help, many of those men might have been dead today. You fully deserve this medal. Wear it with pride."

Shurik fingered his medal as a smile of pleasure began to spread over his face.

"It's beautiful, isn't it?" he said, beaming now.

"Look! Just look at these clippings!" cried Commissar Gogo happily. "Every front-line paper within our radius has an article about Shurik and the hospital." We were gathered in the chief's office for our regular staff meeting. Commissar Gogishvili proudly displayed the results of his publicity efforts.

"I'm thinking of sending these clippings to Moscow," continued the commissar. "Maybe they'll publish them in *Pravda*."

Zina and I left the staff meeting together.

"We've decided on our wedding day," she told me in a low voice.

"When?"

"On the fifth of June. We would like to have you and Dr. Stern be our witnesses."

On the fifth of June the weather was at its best, as if it were doing its utmost to make Zina's wedding day pleasant.

She looked ravishing. It was the first time that I saw her in civilian clothes, for I didn't know her before the war. She was dressed in a white linen dress, trimmed with red grosgrain ribbon. She wore white, high-heeled shoes, and her hair was braided in one thick braid, which fell down her back, reaching below her waist.

Captain Stepanov was in his usual uniform, his right arm in a black silk sling. He called Shurik aside. I saw him give something to Shurik which the boy put into his pocket.

Our little party entered the office of marriage registration. The walls were decorated with prewar posters of happy young couples visiting national resorts on the Black Sea. The clerk, who was to perform the marriage ceremony, was a middle-aged man on crutches. He limped about the room, busily arranging the papers on his desk.

All able-bodied men are at the front, I reflected automatically. *Only women, the crippled, and a few children inhabit Leningrad now.*

The papers were filled out, signed and countersigned by Dr. Stern and me. The clerk stamped them with a rubber stamp and wrote the name of each spouse, registering their new married status.

"By the rights invested in me under the law, I pronounce you man and wife. Congratulations," he declared in a solemn voice.

That was all.

"Wait," said Yuri. "I have something else to add. Shurik, the ring, please."

With a very serious face, Shurik reached into his pocket and handed Yuri a gold ring with a little blue stone, which looked like a sapphire.

"It was my mother's ring," Yuri said. "She gave it to me, for the girl I would marry someday."

"Congratulations to you both," said Dr. Stern, shaking Yuri's good hand and kissing Zina.

"Good luck," I whispered, hugging them; and Shurik, dancing

around them with excitement, chanted "Good luck, good luck!"

Once on the street we parted company. Dr. Stern gave Zina a day off and the newlyweds departed for their new home. Shurik, Dr. Stern and I walked back to the hospital. No holiday for us.

"We'll see you tonight, won't we?" shouted Zina, turning back to us.

"Of course you will. I won't miss a wedding party for anything," chuckled Dr. Stern.

"Neither will I," declared Shurik.

It's hard to believe, but in a few days it will be a whole year that we are at war, I thought, looking out of my window into the pale lavender night sky, studded with air defense balloons. *A whole year. And no end in sight.*

Shurik was sleeping peacefully, snoring gently. I couldn't sleep. I sat at the open window, breathing the warm air, filled with the scent of blooming jasmine and linden. Every year, it was the same. During the white nights I couldn't sleep. There was something beautifully disturbing in our northern nights. The eery light, the soft air, the peculiar quiet of the city, created in one a feeling of great longing, of expectation that something glorious would happen—soon.

There were barely two hours of twilight between sunset and sunrise. One could read in the soft northern lights of the night without the benefit of electricity or candles. I loved this season— as every true Leningrader did. But this year, there was something different in the mood of our white nights. The peaceful, poetic atmosphere was gone. The city lay in the shimmering twilight, waiting, as if ambushed, not daring to breathe. I was disturbed this night, not in the vague, romantic way of previous years, but really disturbed.

Colonel Stern informed me that he received a request from the political branch of the Leningrad Front to release me from my duties at the hospital. I was to be available for a new assignment under the commander of the Red Army Club. Professor Luchinsky must have kept his word and wrote to the Committee on Art Affairs for my transfer from the hospital.

The ambiguity of my feelings bothered me. I longed to be in the theater, working in my own profession, and yet, I had become so accustomed to my hospital, to Dr. Stern, Zina.

And, most important, Shurik. How could I possibly take care of him when I knew I would be assigned to a front-line division, making it impossible for me to return home for weeks at a time! It was different last winter, when I had to be away on the lake. The best thing for Shurik at that time was to be with Dr. Stern, at the hospital. But what about now? The situation in the city improved so much that schools reopened. Shurik ought to be going to school now. He ought not live at the hospital. He must have a normal life. But how could he—with me at the front?

It left only one logical possibility which I couldn't bring myself to accept. He must be put into a children's home. I was given a week to arrange my personal affairs before reporting to my new duty assignment. During this week I was to break the news to Shurik. But how? How could I tell him, after all these months of promising that I would never give him away, how could I tell him that now I must?

Colonel Stern knew about my tormenting dilemma. But he was positive in his own mind of the action I was to take.

"Shurik must be cared for by the proper authorities. He must have a normal life, go to school and be taken out of the city," he told me. "We are heading for another winter of blockade. The child should not be allowed to endure the trials of another winter."

I knew that he was right. This time I had to do as he advised, for Shurik's own good. It was already the second day since I had received my transfer orders, but I still couldn't bring myself to tell Shurik about it.

This morning I was scheduled to go with the Red Army Club truck to the division where I was to work from now on. It was to be a get-acquainted trip, for only two or three hours. I was looking forward to it. It would postpone my "moment of truth" with Shurik.

I looked at him, sleeping so peacefully. How many more days would I have with him—three? Five?

Snezhinka barked in her sleep and made running movements with her paws. *She must be chasing pigeons again,* I thought. Poor Snezhinka had seen few dogs or cats. I was sure she couldn't have remembered her own mother and brother in Kabona. Only pigeons, which reappeared in the city with the coming of summer, provided our dog with the excitement of the chase.

I was utterly depressed by now. I left my post at the window and went to bed. Maybe I would be able to fall asleep.

"Why are you so gloomy?" asked Shurik on our way to the hospital.

"I have a splitting headache," I lied.

I left him at Dr. Stern's office and hurried to the Red Army Club.

I caught a glimpse of Dr. Stern as I ran down the steps. "Did you have a talk with Shurik?" he shouted at me from the upper landing. I shook my head negatively.

The Red Army Club was a large, impressive building, containing a theater, a library and many smaller rooms devoted to special interests and hobbies, such as chess, hunting and fishing. It had an excellent restaurant before the war and a gym for its members.

During the war it became the headquarters for political propaganda and entertainment units. Hundreds of actors worked under the supervision of the club, bringing to the men on the fighting lines a few moments of relaxation.

The lieutenant in charge of my group described to me the hardships to come. The district was constantly under artillery fire. It was in the valley, the Nazis holding the hills above it. "We are there in the palm of their hand," he said, pointing to a map of Leningrad and its environs. Indeed, the Nazis occupied Pushkin, that lovely little town of palaces and parks where our greatest Russian poet went to school. If one were to follow the highway to Pushkin, he would be in enemy hands within less than ten kilometers.

Even closer than in Kabona, I thought. But, somehow, it appeared less frightening to be so near the enemy at this end of the front. Maybe it was because there would be familiar countryside around me. Maybe it was less frightening because it was early summer, the sun was warm and the birds were quarreling in the leafy trees in the garden. Maybe because I had become what they called in official newspaper articles "a seasoned veteran."

We boarded a truck and rolled toward the Narvsky Gates. Our way lay along the broad avenues, past the Kirov plant, which continued to manufacture tanks throughout the worst months of last winter. With horror I observed the devastation of these workers' districts. There was virtually not a block left without a gaping hole, or a demolished building. While in the center of Leningrad, attempts were made to hide the ugly wounds of war, here they were left untouched.

In the center we had most of our bombed buildings covered up with plywood, over which artists had painted windows, doors, balconies and even ornamental decorations, such as caryatids. From a distance these houses looked intact. Here, in this section, so close to the front line, it was no use to hide the destruction. The district and the Kirov plant were among the prime targets of the enemy.

We left the city and immediately began treacherous zigzag maneuvers on the highway. The road had many barricades built across it. The truck had to pass through them as if going through a maze. We could make no detours, for both sides of the road were mined.

Antitank fortifications were on both sides of the highway. They consisted of railroad rails, barbed wire and conical cement blocks, with their sharp ends pointing toward Pushkin, from where the tank attack would come—if it were to come.

Even at Ladoga I had not seen so much security precaution or so many fortifications. Our closeness to the enemy was emphasized by our coming upon a burned-out Nazi tank in the middle of the road. It probably was their reconnaissance vehicle, disabled by our fire and left to burn. But, oh, how close it came to the city. It was within arm's length of a Leningrad streetcar line, just at the place the car would make its loop to return to the city.

We arrived at our destination, a small park, surrounding the suburban Forel Hospital, which became the headquarters of one of our local divisions.

The nerve center of the division was in underground bunkers. Streets and alleys connected one bunker with another. Some of the corridors were well over seven feet high, while the others, the smaller ones, were only waist high, and one had to traverse them in crouching position. Over this underground city camouflage nets were stretched to make it invisible from the air.

The Forel Hospital stood windowless and forlorn. The division used the building for storage, but the commanders intended to move in as soon as the Nazis were pushed farther away.

The bombardment started again. All vehicles were quickly hidden under branches, especially prepared for this purpose. But the enemy shot over our heads, toward the city. For the time being we were safer here than in Leningrad.

Twelve artists were in the group. They started their show at once. The accordionist began to play a lively march. I settled in a corner to watch as the bunker began to fill up with soldiers.

They came straight from their foxholes, dusty, dirty, festooned with grenades, carrying their automatic rifles. They were of all ages—from the very young, boyish eighteen-year-olds to leathery-faced mature men of over forty.

The show began in earnest. There were two dancers from the Leningrad Ballet, dressed in colorful costumes, who danced a lively Ukrainian *gopak*. A singer from the Opera Theater presented a selection of folk songs, accompanying herself on a guitar. Then a magician from the Leningrad Circus performed. Finally a group of actors presented an abridged version of Ostrovsky's comedy, Poverty Is Not a Vice.

The show ended with a song and dance by the whole group, singing *Chastoushki*, humorous ditties, where much fun was made of Hitler's inability to conquer our city. The soldiers loved the show. They clapped their hands wildly, but at a sign from the duty officer they quickly filed-out to let the next group in.

The show was repeated in its entirety at once.

So this will be my new work, I thought. This kind of "artistry" was a far cry from the kind of theater I was used to. But then, who was I to criticize the naiveté of road shows? They brought joy to our fighting men. I would have to wait till better times for more refined productions.

We went back to our truck. The artists grumbled that they were not invited to stay for a meal—always a big bonus—but I was glad that we were returning. I had so much to accomplish before

I would become one of them next Monday.

I arrived at the hospital at dusk. Zina was already gone. Since her marriage, she had moved out of the hospital dormitory and started limited housekeeping in Yuri's flat.

I went straight to the chief's office. Sitting in a chair across from the doctor was Polivanov. He had been allowed to walk for nearly two weeks now, slowly making his way with the help of two canes.

"Good to see you, Comrade Polivanov," I said, disappointed that I didn't catch Dr. Stern alone. I wanted to talk to him about Shurik's future.

"Ah, here you are, my dear, just in time," said the chief pleasantly, inviting me to sit down next to Polivanov. "We were just discussing Sergeant Polivanov's discharge from the hospital. He has recovered so well that we think it's about time he went home to his wife and her cooking. Enough of this dull diet of pine-needle tea, spongy black bread and other blockade delicacies. What he needs now is a wholesome life and rest." The sergeant smiled broadly, nodding his agreement.

Is this what he wants to discuss with me? I thought, surprised at my chief. He knew very well that I was already out of his sphere of command and thus could not contribute to Polivanov's discharge proceedings.

"What we wanted to discuss with you is Shurik's future," continued Dr. Stern. "Sergeant Polivanov has applied for permission to adopt Shurik and take him to Sierénevka when he leaves the hospital in a few days. I wrote a letter requesting that permission be granted. It is the best solution for Shurik, you must agree."

I was stunned. It had all happened so fast. I knew that Polivanov was a fine man, fond of Shurik—but so was everyone.

"What do you say, lieutenant? Don't you think that Shurik

will be happy with my family?" said Polivanov, watching me closely.

"Your family," I said still at a loss to say anything. "Your family——Does your wife know about Shurik?"

"She sure does!" The sergeant smiled broadly. "I wrote her many times about him. She and the kids will be delighted to have Shurik as a member of our family. Even old grandma is waiting for him."

"It is heaven-sent, this solution." Dr. Stern took my hand and looked deep into my eyes. "You must surely realize that Shurik would have to go to an orphanage. Even if you were not re-assigned to theater work and continued at the hospital, Shurik would have to be taken away from you. Don't you see? Your love and your need for him could have denied him a normal and safe life. He must go back to school. He must be taken out of the city."

"Yes, yes, I understand," I stammered.

"The sergeant came to me with the idea of adoption. I thought it was an excellent idea, a most marvelous opportunity for our lad to have a family again. We kept our plan secret until we knew that his request would be met. Then, today, we had a talk with Shurik."

"Yes? What did he say?" I was beginning to comprehend Dr. Stern's moving ahead without me, for he saw that I was im-mobilized.

"Shurik likes the proposition," Dr. Stern said simply.

I felt hurt. *Just like that—he liked the proposition. He was ready to forget me in a flash for some romantic notion of going on a raft along the Kama,* I thought bitterly.

"Shurik is a very intelligent lad," Polivanov broke in. "He realized that if he didn't come with me, he would be placed in a children's home. He knew that there was no other choice for him, with you at the front. So, he chose the lesser of two evils, so to speak," he joked, but his face remained serious.

"When will you be leaving?" I asked.

"In a couple of days. There is a special military evacuation train leaving for Osinovetz. From there, we cross the lake by boat to Kabona, and then on to Vologda by train again, and finally, to Perm and Sierénevka."

"It's in Shurik's best interests," said Dr. Stern. "You ought to feel happy that a man of the sergeant's caliber will bring him up."

Tears welled up in my eyes, but I smiled. I took Polivanov's hand and pressed it. There was a knock at the door. Shurik and Snezhinka burst in. One glance at our trio, and Shurik knew that I was aware of the new development.

"Why didn't you let me prepare her for this shock?" said Shurik to Dr. Stern. "She wouldn't be crying now."

"I'm not crying, darling. Just happy tears. I'm so glad that you'll have a family, a brother and a sister and a mother."

"And a father and even a great-grandmother," he rejoiced. "And Uncle Kolya says that we can take Snezhinka with us."

"We sure can," said Polivanov, looking at Shurik with a fond fatherly smile.

"When will the papers be signed?" I asked Dr. Stern.

"Any day now. Maybe even tomorrow. We don't have much time to spare. The special train leaves on Sunday."

On Sunday, I thought. *The day before I leave for the front. What a strange coincidence of timing? Or was it by design of my kind chief, who wanted to spare me the pain of separation?*

The papers came through and were duly signed. I was at the Red Army Club rehearsing, but my heart was at Dr. Stern's office, wishing that I were there, but happy that I wasn't. Lately I suffered so many mixed feelings.

I gathered Shurik's few possessions which barely covered the bottom of my suitcase. "You'll write to me, won't you?" I kept repeating. Shurik patiently promised to write at least once a month.

Sunday arrived. I took Shurik and Snezhinka to the hospital for the last time. He went from ward to ward saying good-by to the wounded, shaking their hands, wishing them a speedy return to their own families.

He began to call Polivanov "Papa" the moment the sergeant signed his name on the adoption paper. I had a stab of jealousy watching the two of them, but I suppressed it, saying to myself, *It's right for Shurik. I couldn't give him half as much as Polivanov and his family can. It's the best for him.*

The whole staff of the hospital came to the front steps to wish Shurik good luck and a happy life. Dr. Stern and I were to accompany him to the railway station.

A military ambulance arrived to pick us up. Shurik shook hands with the nurses, the aides, the girls from the kitchen, and old Fyodor, who baked him a batch of cookies to take on his long journey. Mamma Lisa cried and kept making the sign of the cross over Shurik and his new father.

Finally we boarded the ambulance and were on our way to the Finlandsky Railroad Station. Shurik nestled against Polivanov as he used to with me.

There, there I go again. Jealous like a child, I thought, angry at myself. *Of course he must nestle against Polivanov. He is his father now. And I am just a friend.*

The train was already full of evacuees. Polivanov and Shurik were given seats near a window, which the sergeant asked the porter to open. The whole train looked dirty and rickety. The station itself was in a sad state. Some of the sidings were destroyed, huge craters yawning in the midst of the railway beds.

The others were full of twisted rails and ties, strewn around like a spilled box of matches. This railroad station was among the favorite objects of Nazi bombardment.

"Don't forget to write us from time to time," Dr. Stern said to Shurik through the open window.

"I won't forget. You, too, must write to me. Promise?"

I nodded, my eyes full of tears, my heart heavy.

Suddenly Shurik bent low through the window, threatening to fall out, and threw his arms around my neck.

"I'll never, never, never forget you," he whispered hotly into my ear and neck. "I always will love you."

A shrill whistle sounded as the train began to move slowly.

"Good-by, good-by!" shouted Shurik to us. "Snezhinka, say good-by to your friends." He hoisted the dog to the window, but she was scared of the noise and ducked right back into the car. Polivanov's smiling face appeared next to Shurik. "Good-by," he yelled to us over the rattle of the wheels.

"Good-by, my Shurik," I whispered. "Have a happy childhood. Go floating on the raft. Good-by." The train was gathering speed.

Dr. Stern took me by the elbow. "Let's go, my dear. Our boy is safe and happy. Let's go." We went to the streetcar together. The colonel held my arm tightly, as if one of us needed support.

"And you are leaving when?" he asked.

"Tomorrow."

"Tomorrow." He appeared to be in a pensive mood. I didn't want to disturb his thoughts.

"Tomorrow," he repeated. "Our Shurik will be well out of danger by tomorrow. Aren't you glad of it?"

"Yes."

"They looked happy together—Polivanov and Shurik. Don't you think so?"

I thought for a moment as the two happy faces appeared in